Marketing in Japan

ROBERT J. BALLON, EDITOR

CONTRIBUTORS

MIHOKO AIHARA, J. Walter Thompson Co., Ltd.

ROBERT J. BALLON, Professor of Economics, Sophia University

JOSÉ M. de VERA, Assistant Professor of Mass Media,
Sophia University

HIDEO GOTŌ, Marketing & Research Supervisor,
J. Walter Thompson Co., Ltd.

YŌTARŌ KOBAYASHI, Director, Fuji-Xerox Co., Ltd.

EUGENE H. LEE, Professor of Law, Sophia University

MITSUO MATSUSHITA, Assistant Professor of Law,
Sophia University

ANDREW M. WATT, J. Walter Thompson Co., Ltd.

TOMOKIYO YAMADA, Management Committee, Creative
Director, J. Walter Thompson Co., Ltd.

Marketing in Japan

The revised edition of
Japan's Market and Foreign Business

ROBERT J. BALLON, *Editor*

PUBLISHED BY

SOPHIA UNIVERSITY · TOKYO

IN COOPERATION WITH

 KODANSHA INTERNATIONAL LTD.

TOKYO, NEW YORK & SAN FRANCISCO

Published by

SOPHIA UNIVERSITY

7 Kioi-chō, Chiyoda-ku

Tokyo 102

in cooperation with

KODANSHA INTERNATIONAL LTD.

2-12-21 Otowa, Bunkyo-ku, Tokyo 112

and

KODANSHA INTERNATIONAL/USA, LTD.

Harper & Row Building, 10 East 53rd Street, New York,

New York 10022, U.S.A.

and

44 Montgomery Street, San Francisco, California 94104,

U.S.A.

World distribution rights: Kodansha International Ltd.
Distributed in Continental Europe by Boxerbooks, Inc., Zurich; in Canada
by Fitzhenry & Whiteside Limited, Ontario.

LC 73-79771

ISBN 0-87011-200-7

JBC 3034-783967-2361

First Printing, 1971

Revised Edition, 1973

Printed in Japan

THE KAWATA PRESS, TOKYO

To

SHIGEO HORIE, international banker,

former Chairman, The Bank of Tokyo,

and President of the Institute for International

Studies and Training (Tokyo),

for his skill in representing his country

in the world community.

Preface

MANY a foreign firm in Japan has been content with its distributor because of a ten percent annual growth in sales... until it has discovered that its distributor has simply been coasting along with the growth of the economy as a whole. In other words, that foreign firm is rapidly losing a place for its own products in the Japanese market unless its growth is in the order of twenty or thirty percent annually—just to keep up with the competition! Nor should blame be directed at the sales people, whose function is, after all, to meet increasing demand. The challenge inherent in this context is a formidable one in Japan. But it is dwarfed by the much more formidable challenge of controlling, to some degree, this continually increasing demand. It is at this point that the marketing manager is hurriedly called for. His counterpart in sales must answer the question: "How much do the Japanese buy?" The marketing manager must answer a more fundamental question: "Why and what do the Japanese buy?"

Hopefully, this book will provide the basic elements for a business-like answer. It goes back to a remark overheard one day: "Fish strike at the same kind of bait that attracts fishermen," a remark that has deceived more than one businessman, particularly in Japan. In the 1960s Japan emerged as a major importer of raw materials; in the 1970s prospects have it that she will emerge as a major importer of finished goods, especially consumer goods, as well as see Tokyo develop into an international capital market. In early 1972 Japan started to advertise herself as an "export market", and agencies such as the Japan External Trade Organization

(JETRO) abruptly switched their main stance from the promotion of exports to that of imports.

Given the homogeneity of the Japanese people and their increasing purchasing power, this 180 degree turn clearly means that international businessmen everywhere must thoroughly re-evaluate their policies toward Japan. Whereas formerly she was often considered as a convenient spot market, a useful outlet permitting product scarcity at home, and as a luxury market for western-style goods, she has today become an increasingly decisive market in international competition. Marketing strategy must be revised accordingly.

Like our other books on business in Japan, this one is the result of discussions in the international management development seminars sponsored by the Socio-Economic Institute of Sophia University (Tokyo). Here, experienced foreign and Japanese executives involved in international operations in Japan have discussed, among many other topics, the challenge of marketing in Japan. Some of the executives were successful; others were just struggling along; and still others, not the minority, were in the process of, let us say, revising their market strategy and tactics. Most of them felt that they had not initially been given adequate opportunity and time to prepare themselves for their Japanese marketing tasks: they would have wished for a greater advance familiarity with the specifics of Japan's challenge, besides national statistics, past records of their company's performance in Japan, and . . . the difficulties of communicating with their Japanese staff. They were told that setting up in Japan is more than accommodating one's strategy to government policies (as if a totally free entry into the Japanese market would necessarily spell resounding success); that the Japanese consumer is changing his attitudes and taste (not necessarily, however, in the direction of "their" product); that in advertising copy English words are fine, but that they should not be their own English words or those of English-speaking customers; that their increase in turnover should not match the

Preface

standards of the home office, but those of their Japanese competitors; and so on and on.

This book would not have come to light, however, without the professional advice of Dr. Kinichiro Saito, President of the J. Walter Thompson (Japan) Co., who enlisted his staff for some key chapters. Contributors and editor join in expressing their gratitude to Dr. Kenneth Scholes for patiently going over the manuscript and making it into a smoothly flowing text, testifying thereby that marketing, even in Japan, starts with correct and clear language.

THE EDITOR
February 1973

CONTENTS

Part I

SETTING UP IN JAPAN

Part II

THE JAPANESE CONSUMER

Contents

Part III

MARKETING STRATEGY FOR JAPAN

List of Exhibits

Part I

SETTING UP IN JAPAN

CHAPTER ONE

"Our Marketing Man in Japan . . ."

ROBERT J. BALLON

*Discovering Japan and the Japanese market—Becoming part of
the vertical society—Changing with changing Japan*

ANY international corporations have long relied on inter-
mediaries for their sales in Japan, but in the last few
years a drastic change has occurred. A new dimension has
been given to Japanese marketing through the emergence of "our
man in Japan". For ages observed at a distance, Japan was like the
moon until man finally landed on it. For years, if not decades,
figures of sales in Japan were listed side by side with sales in India,
Turkey, or Zambia; all they meant was that "our products are
also sold in Japan". A double assumption was, and is still, prevalent. One has to do with the product, the other with strategy:

1) "Our products are universal." That is, American toothpaste
    is displayed in street-stalls in Calcutta; a computer is attend-
    ed by barefooted programmers in Kathmandu; Chanel No. 5
    is as much appreciated in Tokyo as in New York; and so on.

2) "Customers are customers everywhere." Hence the con-
    clusion that a successful campaign in Europe must also be
    successful in Japan, that a Japanese housewife must also pre-
    fer the large economy size, and so on.

If such assumptions were stated company policy, they might be
less dangerous than when they are implicit judgements screwed into

[3]

the brains of decision-makers at the home office. The ultimate authority for such assumptions is usually adduced as "experience" gathered while enjoying the lavish hospitality of a Japanese associate. The fact is that international corporation headquarters, notwithstanding the new label of "multinational," hunt for universal norms applicable to Japan as well as to other markets. The norm most commonly invoked is "It's good for them!" Not so long ago a Japanese businessman in a private conversation compared such an attitude (and he did not exclude the Japanese themselves) to the colonial attitude, justified by the need to bring civilization to the natives. Marketing overseas, like other functions of international business, is still readily rationalized in terms like "It's good for them!" That there are some differences is not denied, but agents are supposed to take care of the differences.

Matters improved somewhat with representation on the spot. Up until the end of the fifties "our man in Japan" was in many instances an old China hand, so-called, transferred to Japan because "Japan is like China," or a second-generation Japanese *(nisei)* hired because "he speaks Japanese." In the sixties, headquarters started sending out people with specific backgrounds in marketing; they are now back at headquarters, hopefully not maimed promotion-wise by their two or three years in Japan. It seems that in the seventies home offices more and more frequently assign their best man in marketing to secure a grip on the Japanese market. Meanwhile, one year in Japan looks like three to five years at home, and, while sales figures increase, the market share slips. To speak bluntly, in Japan a sales turnover increasing by only 10% means that the corporation is rapidly losing its market share; the "good" figures hover between 20 and 30% a year. These latter figures apply in the West to some successful new product, but in Japan they should apply to the total market basket of the corporation.

The marketing expert, now assigned to Japan, was probably informed a few weeks in advance. He spent them packing household goods, saying goodbye to friends, and left either puzzled by the new assignment or plainly confident that Japan was no match for his wits. He might have been shown the company file on Japan so as to take note of the names and addresses of a few important contacts; he might have had a look at the company library only to find that "Marketing in Japan" had no entry; he might even have paid a courtesy call on the executives previously assigned to Japan. In any case, he has just now stepped off the plane at Tokyo International Airport. That is where we meet him, as he is about to enter into the preparatory phase of his duties in Japan, the discovery of the Japanese market; it will last as long as his instinctive reaction is to keep his head "above water" to see where he is going. If all goes well, we may find him still around during the second phase, the formative one, when he plunges head under water into the swift whirlpools of the Japanese market. Later, he will emerge again to enter into the innovative phase of the market.

Discovering Japan and the Japanese market

CONCERN about the product is for research and production people; our man is primarily interested in the customer. He has been heard referring jokingly to the axiom, "The customer is always right"; now he is confronted with the "Japanese" customer. Shots have immunized him against cholera and the like; they did not—nor does the distance, as a matter of fact—immunize him against home-office assumptions: he has marketed our products and will market them in Japan, and he has learned a lot about "the" customer. One difference will soon emerge. Japan is still the only industrialized country outside of the western hemisphere. As a customer, the United States male differs from the United States female and the Swiss townsman from the Swiss highlander; but why on earth assume that the United States male and the Swiss townsman, or any other western combination, are paragons of the

Japanese *sarariman,*[1] a postwar breed of consumer as "Japanese" in his characteristics as the samurai or the geisha? In regard to Japan, there is truly no point of reference in space or time. The result is that to our man the peculiarities of the Japanese consumer appear, at first, simply exotic.

This is not to say that exoticism brought him to Japan; it was the irresistible lure of 100,000,000 people with an average annual income of $2,000! Still, if you ask him after a few weeks in Japan where he meets the true Japan, his answer is bound to be the equivalent of: "In the gardens of Kyoto" . . . The encounter does not take place in his office, where he is surrounded with the paraphernalia of the home office. It does not take place at his home either, which does not compare in any way with that of the average Japanese and for which he pays a monthly rent equivalent to four to five months' salary of the average Japanese employee. He develops, however, a certain familiarity with Japan through the written language: though he is unable to read it, he is proud to *see* the company's name written in Japanese and to oversee promotional material being translated. In fact, he makes it a point to check by himself the Japanese translation . . . in English, of course! At any rate, the unreadable writing carries a familiar message. But he still jumps at the inevitable "yes" that answers any of his questions and later remembers that "yes" stands for "I heard you," not "I agree."

The result of all these observations and many more is that to some foreigners the Japanese are likable, to others indifferent at best, and to many queer. To few foreigners, however, does it occur that they themselves may be queer, *hen na gaijin* ('queer foreigner'), as the Japanese say. As time goes by, the situation may get unbearable: our man is one in a thousand, and the remaining 999 are Japanese! Here is where the exotic approach may be misleading. To be the foreign exception (1/1,000) to the Japanese rule (999/1,000) may

---

[1] See Ezra F. Vogel, *Japan's New Middle Class,* Berkeley: University of California Press, 1963.

suit western individualism; it is of little help to the marketing man. The exotic outlook is in the mind of the foreigner, not in the mind of the Japanese customer. The basic error is that, except for these exotic trappings, the Japanese customer is assumed to be no different from any other customer. It is like Japanese copy: the marketer cannot read his own advertising, but he thinks he knows what it says, and he thinks he knows what the customer wants. His admiration for the gardens of Kyoto pleases the Japanese, but they find it odd that he does not realize that the office building in which he works is as much and as truly Japan as the gardens.

The Japanese himself contributes to this exotic outlook by his praise of western technology (he may be more reserved when it comes to western culture!) and by adopting externally many western ways. Driving a car is westernization to the foreigner; to the *sarariman* it means simply that he can now afford that new means of transportation. Instant foods are another sign of westernization, but to the Japanese housewife they are more convenient than the usual perishable foods. Baseball, introduced before the turn of the century, is now as much a national sport to the Japanese as to the American. The latest symbol of westernization is the skyscraper, but where in the West has a skyscraper ever been built to resist an average of one or two earthquakes a week?

After his first contact with the Japanese market, the foreigner has still not learned much that is helpful to a long-term marketing effort. Meanwhile, however, he may have succeeded in selling to the Japanese some "exotic" products, i.e., his own! Such success has a positive value when it means insight into the dynamics of the Japanese market as a whole, if not of the national economy itself. It encourages a closer look at Japan. Twirling his executive chair, our man faces a shelf of books on Japan. His readings now gain a glow they did not convey when, on the day of his assignment to Japan, he picked up some volumes dealing with Japan. Some comments stand out, and are relished. A keen observer of Japan has, for example, demonstrated conclusively that from 1868 to 1936 the largest part of the resources of Japan went to her people, not so much for the sake of their welfare as for the sake of economic development. Speaking of the consumer, the same author stresses repeatedly that, because of the individualized tastes of the Japanese, very few products had found a national market.[2] This past throws light on the present. Another observer, in a journalistic vein, turns to today's Japan and expresses his surprise at the modernity of Tokyo; but hastens to add:

> "... on the back of these people there is not one gram of Japanese cotton, not a single thread of wool coming from Japanese sheep. The metal of these cars, of these coaches, of these rails, of these bridges, has come totally from far away countries in the form of ore. The gasoline for these vehicles was imported in the form of crude oil almost to the last drop. The rubber of these tires comes from abroad, etc."[3]

Such is the material evidence of the present harbinger of Japan's role in future years. As the marketer pages through such volumes and others on culture, arts, and sociology, he will hardly resist the temptation to allude to such literary pursuit in his reports to the home office, where somebody will shake his head: "Our man in Tokyo has come under the spell!"

Then come the first experiences in business dealings. Our man is baffled at the cost of doing business in Japan; not only are his personal costs higher than at home, but all the rest seems to follow the same principle: representation costs, advertising, promotion, and so on. He also begins to feel, as he puts it, that there are definitely too many Japanese: at any time, anywhere, there is always somebody else—and there may be many—involved in whatever goes on.

---

[2] William W. Lockwood, *The Economic Development of Japan—Growth and Structural Change, 1868–1938*, Princeton: Princeton University Press, 1954, *passim*.

[3] Robert Guillain, *Japon, Troisième Grand*, Paris: Le Seuil, 1969, p. 85.

Chapter One. "Our Marketing Man in Japan . . ."

Take distribution: given so many middlemen, it is no wonder that products are substantially marked up when they reach the ultimate user and price control is practically out of the question. What is at stake is more than a business problem. Any dealing with and among Japanese, business and otherwise, rarely takes place in the form of a man-to-man talk. To ask for a direction in the street results in several passers-by seemingly reviewing the plight of the lost person before the one who was initially asked volunteers the information, probably known all along. Marriages arranged by *nakōdo* ('go-between') are still the majority; labor disputes are turned over to the Labor Relations Commission well before normal negotiation methods are exhausted; and other disputes, even brought to court, are settled outside the court with the help of a third party. At the office, few communications are transmitted directly; relays are always necessary. Decision-making consists in progressively reaching a consensus and then having it endorsed as a decision. And so on and so on. In Japan, there is always somebody else involved; the third party is a social institution.

An identical pattern is followed by the distribution system: several layers of wholesalers and dealers must be expected in almost any product line. By tradition, they have not been entrusted only with the physical distribution and storage of goods supplied by the manufacturer; they have also been involved in financing the distribution itself and today contribute enormously to re-creating debt-financing possibilities at every level. Too often they have been described as a harmful screen between the manufacturer and the market; but, as well described by their traditional name *ton-ya* (literally 'house to ask'), their main function has always been to relay, on the one side to the manufacturer and on the other to the customer, needed market information. Until the advent in recent years of the mass-production market, distribution was never considered a special sector of the economy. Manufactured goods were traded almost in the same spirit as perishable goods supplied locally and displayed in the local market place. It is only in the last decade

[9]

that government publications, as plans issued by the Economic Planning Agency, started to devote explicit attention to distribution. Even today the same market psychology prevails in a very successful Japanese institution, the general trading firm, like the Mitsui or Mitsubishi Trading Co.; it is also exemplified in the fact that many large firms have their own trading companies as wholly-owned subsidiaries.

The foreign marketer may feel that he should not allow the distribution system to grow fat on his products. Condemning it from the viewpoint of economics, he has a spontaneous reaction: to bypass it all and sell directly. How foolish of him, if he thinks that this "rational" approach requires a western mind; the Japanese mind can contrive it as well. What hinders its adoption is usually expressed in terms of labor cost and cash flow, both problems directly related to the dual structure of the Japanese industry. The salary system prevalent in large firms (and expected in foreign firms operating in Japan) ties in with lifelong employment security *(shūshin koyō)* and the consideration of length of service *(nenkō joretsu)* in the automatic progression of individual salaries. Labor cost thus becomes a fixed cost.[4] In order to fulfil this expectation, a general feature of the Japanese industrial system is subcontracting *(shita uke)* to smaller firms where employment conditions are perforce more flexible and where labor mobility exists. The same is true in distribution: instead of having the sales force on his own payroll, the manufacturer leaves sales to a related firm; and so further down the line of distribution. In addition, financing is directly determined by the prevailing social interdependence of all units in industrial society. The perennial headache of Japanese enterprises, large and small, is the shortage of liquid funds; and the manufacturer is thus most anxious to spread and share distribution costs as widely as possible, compounded as they are by

---

[4] See Robert J. Ballon (ed.), *The Japanese Employee,* Tokyo: Sophia-Tuttle, 1969, chapter six.

such common practices as promissory notes, debt financing, and the consignment system.

But let us return to our man and his economic rationality. To sell directly is his privilege, if he is willing to foot the bill. Let him be carried away by a missionary zeal to show the Japanese that it can be done. Once the breakthrough has been financed successfully, he thinks, the Japanese will throng through it! The point remains that to sell directly in Japan is often less a matter of market strategy than of financial backing.[5] Success outside of "normal" Japanese ways, i.e., in terms of economic rationality, is possible . . . at a cost. In the case of direct selling, for example, the financial cost may be substantial and worth it, but a dangerous liability may also be incurred in the process. What helps sales in the short run may damage the corporate image, a vital marketing consideration, in the long run. The social environment of marketing will accept the novelty only at its own pace.

Having taken the courageous decision to bypass the middleman or, for that matter, the equally courageous decision to use the middleman, our man has still another party to face, the omnipresent government. If it is not this section of the Ministry of International Trade and Industry (MITI), it is another; if it is not the Ministry of Agriculture, it is the Ministry of Welfare; and if it is not the Customs Bureau, it is the Fair Trade Commission. Meanwhile, little help is obtained by turning to Japanese colleagues. Even when they themselves complain against the ever present government, the astute listener senses that viewpoints, theirs and his, do not meet. He, the foreigner, condemns middlemen, go-betweens, government—all of them—as "outsiders" who "interfere". The Japanese, in fact, consider them as "insiders" who "participate".

Our man in Japan is now through what we called the preparatory

---

[5] Our argument should not be understood as a justification for the complexity of the Japanese distribution pattern. Streamlining is imperative and in progress, as shown in other chapters.

stage, which is concerned with the discovery of Japan and of the Japanese market. He is about to enter bravely the second phase, the formative one whereby, it is hoped, his marketing effort will integrate with the vertical society so characteristic of Japan.

Becoming part of the vertical society

IN the formative stage our man puts his head under water in the sense that he must guide his marketing effort into the mainstream of the Japanese market. So far, he has been swimming with his head above water to see where he was going and what it was all about. What he has seen so far was a market expanding at twice or three times the speed of other markets he may have known. He now considers another strategy: "If you can't beat them, join them." This is the formative stage of marketing in Japan. Thus, holding his breath, he lets himself sink into . . . the Japanese community: his marketing effort sinks into Japan's vertical society.

The encounter with the third-party syndrome occurs at the root of a further deepening of understanding cultural variances. Anthropologists, Japanese and other, have pointed out that Japanese society is a *tate shakai* ('vertical society'), meaning that social relations are more vertical than horizontal.[6] What difference does it make to the marketer?

First instance: horizontal relationship

Manufacturer ⟷ Middlemen ⟷ Customers

In this instance, the one prevailing in the West, the three factors, manufacturer, middleman, and customer, are on the same level and have each an independent reality; they are given practically identical importance, modified only by their specific function. The result is

---

[6] See, for example, Chie Nakane, *Japanese Society*, Berkeley: University of California Press, 1970.

that in such a relationship the factors are replaceable; the relationship comes to life only in the product concerned. It may be regarded as a good example of so-called economic rationality.

Second instance: the vertical relationship

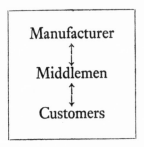

Manufacturer

Middlemen

Customers

In this case, the relationship is rooted in a given hierarchy of human rapport; what counts is not so much the product as the persons involved, the relationship itself. The factors are participating factors; their reality as factors comes from their participation in the relationship. As so clearly indicated by the forms and nuances of his language, the Japanese is almost never speaking to another at the same level; he speaks either to a "superior" or to an "inferior", but without necessarily implying subordination or superiority. It is all determined by the symbiosis of Japanese society. The hierarchy of the vertical relationship is not determined from the outside, nor is it imposed from above; it is the actual working of the relationship, namely of the people involved. It would be erroneous to construe it along the lines of western individualism. It has been noted repeatedly that even in modern Japan expressions of individualism *(kojin-shugi)* are negative in the sense that they are negations of loyalty to the group *(giri)*. Elaborating on his research among the residents of the "Mamachi" district, Professor Ezra F. Vogel writes:

"If one accepts the Kantian view that morality implies duty, Mamachi residents do not consider individualism as a kind of morality—they do not conceive of individualism as the responsibility of a person to be true to his own ideals. Individual-ism does not imply a sense of oughtness or responsibility, but rather it is seen as the right and privilege of an individual to look out for his own interests even against the interests of the group. To the extent that individualism brings with it any duty at all, it is simply the obligation of the person in power to permit a measure of freedom to the person lower in the hier-archy . . . Few people in Mamachi consider it a higher morality to be concerned more with one's own benefit than with the welfare of one's group."[7]

The vertical relationship is thus expressed negatively by lack of individualism and positively by the hierarchical order. The way it works in the distribution system is no different. But as manifested in marketing it is more immediately obvious in the industrial market; but it is just as active, though much less obvious, in the consumer market. Some instances will illustrate the point.

Since the relationship is so deeply personal, it is not surprising that subjective considerations seem to predominate. Even when specific terms like *giri* ('loyalty') and *ninjō* ('empathy') are not specifically used (this being more the case in the Tokyo area than in the Osaka area), the values involved are there. It can be clearly seen in the lack of uniformity in regard to the need and the form of business contracts.

---

[7] Vogel, *op. cit.*, pp. 147–148. Yanaga writes: "One of the characteristics of Japanese society is the existence of a number of rather exclusive groupings. Most of these are primary groups in which intimacy is achieved through submersion of individuality to the extent of not even using individual names." (Chitoshi Yanaga, *Big Business in Japanese Politics*, New Haven: Yale University Press, 1968, p. 15.) A striking example is given by Dore: "The question: 'What religion are you in your family?' produces in over-whelming proportions the reply 'Buddhism,' which refers to the fact that the family has a family temple on whose services it calls if need be. On the other hand, the question: 'Do you personally have any religious belief?' produces eighty-eight noes out of a hundred." (Ronald Dore, *City Life in Japan*, Berkeley: University of California Press, 1967, p. 329.)

". . . In the case of this trading company, there was no basic contract for the sale of machinery and electrical appliances, but the sale of fuel, coal and iron ore was governed by basic contracts.

. . . Medium and small companies are still reluctant to use contracts with many clauses, and this resistance exists in some large companies as well. A majority of the employees with sales departments emphasize the importance of clear specifications particularly when the transaction involves unfamiliar products. They feel, however, that detailed legalistic provisions unnecessarily hurt the feelings of their business partners. They believe that problems can and should be solved through negotiation based on mutual trust and the personal relations between the parties. Although they are aware of possible disastrous consequences that may arise from the lack of clauses, they strongly feel that the harmonious relations with their customers and partners should not be impaired by hard clauses that may be useful only in rare instances."[8]

The Japanese are, therefore, most concerned about letting the contract remain "flexible". The same attitude prevails in regard to pricing. With not much exaggeration it could be said that pricing is an open-end affair for the seller as well as for the buyer. More than anywhere else, it is difficult in Japan to form a precise idea (if one wanted to!) of the cost of a product because of the many unaccountable or not properly accounted for "human" commitments resulting from the vertical relationship. This unaccountability is rooted in the basic feature of the employment situation in Japan, making the labor cost a practically fixed cost, forcing a greater flexibility in pricing. This is not to deny that in recent years many manufacturers have increased their control over the distribution

---

[8] J. Toshio Sawada, *Subsequent Conduct and Supervening Events*, Tokyo: University of Tokyo Press, 1968, pp. 199 and 200.

network. Price control, however, even where allowed by the Fair Trade Commission, seems to be only one aspect of the deeper urge to expand the scale of operations and thus better qualify for bank credit.

If contracts are "flexible" and prices are "flexible", what on earth restrains the buyer-seller relationship from running wild? The most effective constraint is institutional. It looks like brand loyalty, but it is not. Brand loyalty is consumer-oriented; in Japan it is rather the "loyalty" of the seller to his own image as recognized by the public at large, i.e., "Japan". This is the reason why institutional advertising is playing a greater role in Japan; the advertiser is less concerned about the product image than about the institutional image which, however, is not limited to the corporate image (whereby the firm is considered as an individual entity), but implies the popular image of the industrial grouping or the industry to which the firm belongs. It may well be one of the reasons why advertising agencies are still largely limited to the role of space-brokers; the client performs all the other functions of advertising by himself. Another institutional dimension arises from environmental circumstances. For example, in department stores the customers expect the prices to be fixed and the purchases dated by a rubber stamp on the wrapping; on the supply side, on the other hand, endless negotiations take place and much *giri* is displayed. In the chain stores direct suppliers are allowed to quote only a final price, but most perishable items are handled on a concession basis allowing flexible pricing.

The vertical relationship greatly influences market strategies, since fundamentally the demonstration effect, if any, is less communicated from one individual to another than somehow generated from within the group: the effect is slower in building up, but once on the move it spreads wider and deeper. One of the results is that market segmentation must be approached with great caution. By isolating one sector, the misleading assumption may be made that thereby a certain independence is restored. This is not so, because for one thing independence was never there and for another the market relationship is but one of many more relationships. The foreign marketer should therefore be careful not to consider the market as composed of discrete units to which mass production now offers his product as a "common denominator". To crowd out a competitor is done by the Japanese themselves; it seems to be condoned readily as a manifestation of distress selling; it will be put in a most unfavorable light by any other circumstance.

When the product is not, in final analysis, what clinches the marketing relationship, it should be expected that after-sale services are easily neglected on the one hand and that the new model is readily purchased on the other. The replacement is determined less by some technical superiority of the new feature added than by the higher step in social recognition of the product resulting from the addition of the new feature. The introduction of an entirely new product or marketing method encounters, however, little resistance on one condition, that the new relationship somehow embodies the "proper" standards. This is to say that the innovation should not be such as to place the newcomer ahead of everybody else (unless at a very considerable risk that will slowly become apparent). The ideal position is to be just one step ahead. In an old industry it means that expected and traditional relationships are neither cut nor ignored and that in a new industry considerable attention is devoted to building up relationships stressing the communality in the making rather than protecting a monopoly position. Both policies understandably extend well beyond whatever success the new product may know in the short run.

It is, therefore, scarcely surprising that Japanese marketers are much concerned about an overall control over the marketing relationship. In true Japanese fashion, this is not attempted primarily by legalistic means such as resale price maintenance or the like; the main effort is aimed at controlling the human dynamics of the relationship. A commonly used method is the establishment of a network of club-like organizations initiated by the manufacturer, as found in cosmetics and pharmaceuticals in the consumer market and duplicated in a way by groupings in the industrial market. The basic idea is to obtain social control: selected distributors are given special privileges; selected retailers obtain franchises; customers are organized in clubs. The entire network is then cemented together by public-relations magazines, special events, sponsored trips, and so on that reinforce the common bond. It explains why the soft-sell approach is overwhelmingly preferred to the hard-sell. It even appears that these marketing techniques, as practiced more and more in today's Japan, are more directly than in other industrialized countries an immediate contribution to ushering in the "Information Era", putting to full use the high rate of literacy of the Japanese public.

The control of the vertical relationship, as stated repeatedly, is possible only from within; this is where the foreign marketer easily fails. He may be simply "absorbed" by the relationship: sales may be satisfactory for the moment, but marketing is nil. It happens most easily when products are put into the hands of an exclusive dealer, or the maintenance of one's own trademark is neglected, or products are allowed to be distributed under a different brand name. Some promising marketing efforts have been defeated for no other reason than a lack of perspective on the dynamics of the vertical society. A most dangerous assumption is made, for example, when the challenge is expected to come from a competitor of the size of the home-office operations. Quite often the deadly competitor turns out to be of smaller size, much smaller size, taking off on what could be thought of as a suicide mission![9]

Returning now to our man in Japan, we may find him convinced that the only way to control the vertical relationship is from within . . . but wondering how to get in! Two fairly simple rules

[9] Looking back at prewar Japan and attempting to draw some inference for the industrialization of Far East developing countries, Lockwood wrote: "The Englishman as a foreign entrepreneur in India, like the Dutchman in Java and the American in the Philippines, found it both difficult and less profitable to adapt to new purposes the traditional fabric of industrial organization. The Japanese businessman was working in*

of conduct are codified by Japanese etiquette and will prove in-
dispensable: to be introduced and to meet many relevant people—
two simple rules that our man, pressed by time, might neglect.

One could well compare Japan to an exclusive club where no
newcomer is accepted without introduction by a member. No
contact will be initiated without making sure that proper introduction has been obtained; for very important matters, the introduction must be made in person. Even, at some later stage, any new major
development will be presented with reference to a third party. To
be introduced in Japan is not a mere formality, notwithstanding
what the foreigner may feel about the practice or its usefulness. As
much as possible, the introduction should be made by a known third
party, and that means a Japanese individual, or a top management
member of a Japanese firm, known by the Japanese partner. It may
well be a competitor. The purpose of the introduction, in the business world, is not so much to establish a business relation as, more
fundamentally, to establish a human relation. It attempts, therefore,
to make the newcomer part of the given social network. Supposing
that he has been properly introduced, he must then make himself
known. It will not be enough to exchange the ritual *meishi* ('business
card'); the Japanese businessmen do that among themselves all day
long! The foreigner may resent it, but he will certainly be asked
whether he is married, how many children he has, and so on. This
is not vain curiosity and invasion of privacy; these social dimensions
help to situate the stranger in a social context with which the
Japanese is not familiar. Another common question: "Does your
family live in Japan?" is simply an attempt to relate the stranger to
the Japanese environment. All such information is known by Japanese about one another, because they are known to each other much
less through an "I-and-Thou" relationship than by participation in

*his own country and among his own people. And his activities were subject to surveil-
lance and control of a government which, while not unduly preoccupied with the interest
of the small fellow—to put it mildly—was a regime independent of foreign domination and concerned with Japan's own autonomous development." (Lockwood, *op. cit.*,
p. 214.)

common social relations. This is also why so much business entertainment takes place in Japan; the "rational" business relationship is not sufficient to establish the expected human rapport.

As long as proper introduction has not taken place and one has not made himself known, the relationship cannot properly progress. And let it be made clear once more, it is not the product, even a well-known product, and it is not the foreign company's name, even a world-renowned one, that constitute proper introductions. The human rapport is brought about by people, not by things!

The second rule of conduct has to do with the proper social intercourse. The foreign marketer, often obsessed by the purpose of selling his product, tends to look for the quickest possible way to dispose of it and then move to another prospect. He gets impatient at meeting so many Japanese, among whom none, it seems, has the power to make the decision to buy. However, the community spirit makes it practically impossible to meet only one Japanese. To repeat the same presentation over and over again to different groups all representing the same institutional customer is no waste of time; let us say that it is not until almost everybody in the organization has had the chance to be exposed to the product and, more so, to its marketer, that a purchase can be considered. A quick sell almost inevitably will be a last sell. It is not different in regard to the individual customer: no logical presentation triggers conviction, but the same message in varied circumstances may well do so.

There is no sure-fire approach to the Japanese market; it wants to assimilate, not to be sold, a new product. Therefore, both the product and its marketer have first to become part of the environment. Exceptions are often quoted; but once assimilation has been achieved, it is easy to overlook the time and efforts that were lavishly spent by the marketer. The "conditioning-to-Japan" process is a tricky one; numerous attempts at japanizing a foreign product have turned into dismal failures. The Japanese like and go for what is foreign, BUT not as the foreigner sees it; they refer it to their own categories, the categories of the Japanese community. Most successful foreign marketing ventures in Japan have made allowance for this assimilation period, both in time and money. The successful way to start in Japan is . . . in the red, often for a period of two or three years. It is like jumping on a streetcar in motion: it is most dangerous to do so from a standing position and safer after running alongside for a while. To jump on the Japanese bandwagon travelling at the speed of 10% annual growth requires an alert organization.

The two rules of conduct have been presented primarily in terms of personal conduct of the foreign marketer, but they apply also to the institutional behavior of his organization, the local operations and the home office. The demands of marketing in Japan are not measured only in dollars and time; they must also be measured in social values involved on both sides. Hopefully, marketing will be one more means not to negate, but to reconcile cultural differences. From the viewpoint of international marketing, acceptance and participation in the Japanese community do not occur at the cost of losing one's "foreign" identity. Rather, they occur through genuine contribution to the marketing relationship. At the risk of paradox, we might say that, although such a contribution originates outside the community, it is provided from within. A marketing expert stated one day that, ideally speaking, the name of the product should be written in *katakana*, the syllabic alphabet used to transcribe foreign words, but the name of the company should be written in *kanji*, the Chinese characters.[10] It was considered as a victory at the home office when the name of the joint venture was finally agreed upon as "Caterpillar-Mitsubishi", but the Japanese know the company as "Mitsubishi-Caterpillar"!

Having survived the ordeals of the preparatory phase, when he discovered Japan, and the formative phase, when he started to become part of the vertical society, our man in Japan is now about to enter the innovative phase that consists soberly in changing with changing Japan.

[10] Remark made by Dr. K. Saito.

Changing with changing Japan

THROUGH the previous phase, the foreign marketer has felt the pulse of the Japanese community: a social reality that does not bind together independent units (individuals), but molds interdependent units (members). Statistics, therefore, that are based on a mere compilation of individual reactions do not convey the all-important point that the "community" is more than "large numbers", that the community is constitutive of the Japanese individual.

The Japanese community is far from static, and this is to the liking of the foreign marketer who considers himself as a factor of change and hopes to induce a change that will turn the tide in his favor. What does it mean to compound his change on changing Japan? At the risk of some crude over-simplification, may it not be said that change for the foreign marketer too often boils down to changing brand A for brand B? In other words, something is removed and something else is put in its place. However, the Japanese market does not change in the sense of replacing, but only in the sense of adding—a much simpler process, in fact. To replace implies cutting off an existing relationship and thereby disturbing, if not ruining, the delicate balance of established human rapport. To add, even at the cost of a temporary contradiction (in terms of economic rationality), leaves the old relationship untouched, while a new relation is introduced around which, given time, a new equilibrium will be formed. Here again we find a perfect expression of the vivid concern of the Japanese for flexibility. The phenomenon is nothing new; it has characterized modern Japan from the start.

"The natural capability of the Japanese economy to mix the styles of its capital formation is one of the most important determinants of its successful growth. Japan brought to economic development a built-in resistance to the corroding influence of the demonstration effect—the deep commitment to a traditional economy that has continued to be productive to this day. The modern sector has succeeded because it climbed onto the shoulders of the traditional sector."[11]

The community, and the market for that matter, is not a closed one; on the contrary, a continuous process of assimilation seems long to have characterized Japan. Fifteen centuries ago Chinese civilization was assimilated, one century ago western industrialization, and today western technology. At no point of history, however, has Japan lost her identity as Japan; on the contrary, Japan has become more Japan by each new assimilation. What the outsider may construe at first sight as a refusal of the new is in fact only a delay: adoption can take place right away, assimilation requires time. How much time? Such a question does not make much more sense than to ask how much time it takes for a steak to be digested and assimilated. This is not so much a matter of minutes or hours as one of metabolism. Such is also the position of the foreign marketer: is he or is he not in the bloodstream of the community? But the Japanese community should not be looked at as a monolith; it is a cluster of smaller communities (e.g., enterprises), themselves broken down in smaller groups (e.g., sections, school-cliques). It is like a living cell composed of molecules, themselves composed of atoms, and so on. Change, or better, assimilation, may take place in any of the molecules or atoms, while next to it another molecule or atom assimilates something else. Interaction is constant and compounding.

"The functioning of the Japanese social system is based on interpersonal relationships, maintained through a variety of groupings, both vertical and horizontal. The former are exemplified primarily, though not exclusively, by the *oyabun-kobun*

11 Henry Rosovsky, *Capital Formation in Japan, 1868–1940*, New York: The Free Press of Glencoe, 1961, p. 53.

relationship . . . (a type of father-son or parent-child relationship). Horizontal relationships are represented by kinship or
marriage ties *(keibatsu)* and bonds resulting from the sharing
of common experiences—such as going through the same
school, college, or university *(gakubatsu)*, coming from the
same prefecture *(kyōdobatsu)*, growing up together in the
same neighborhood, belonging to the same club, or being born
in the same year. In actual situations the vertical and horizontal
ties are usually intertwined and are not separable."[12]

Such is the social dynamism that pervades the market. No other
market in the world has sustained over more than a decade an
annual growth rate of 10% in real terms. Such a rate would probably blow apart the Japanese economy and Japanese society if it
was not for the community, the groups within the group. The rapid
change can be traced as well at the level of the industrial customer
as at that of the end-consumer: to both, change means expansion,
addition.

The drive to expand manifests itself in the industrial groupings:
no firm truly stands by itself (how could it, since the debt-equity
ratio averages eighty to twenty?). Interlocking directorates and
similar relations are usually explained in terms of the perennial
thirst for funds, but this thirst itself results from the urge to expand
which consequently swells the group. Marketing of industrial goods
must therefore be directed less at individual firms than at clusters
of firms. It will greatly help the marketer to trace the origin of
unloaded executives and equipment (a common practice of larger
firms in regard to related smaller firms) and know the life history
of managers and machinery. The marketer may hit the jackpot
when he succeeds in localizing within this cluster the purchasing
function, which often also operates in a financing capacity.

This urge to expand finds a sort of common denominator in the

[12] Yanaga, *op. cit.*, pp. 12–13.

government. In postwar years the national policy has been very much to strengthen the industrial foundations of the economy: heavy and chemical industries. It has given Japan the third largest GNP in the world. Now attention starts to get focused on the per capita income; this is the latest national policy. It would therefore be a dangerous mistake on the part of the foreign marketer to try to fence off a portion of the market and consider it as private hunting grounds. In crowded Japan profitable wildlife is generated only in the national reserves.

Within the enterprise, a similar phenomenon is observed. "Where is the man in charge of purchasing in this company?" is a question that does not make much sense to a Japanese. Even when the purchasing function has been clearly circumscribed on the company's organization chart, it remains a function of the whole, not however by a specific delegation of authority (except of course for smaller purchases). The foreign marketer may extol the inner qualities of his industrial product; the Japanese industrial customer takes a different view: he somehow relates the product to the overall development of the firm; its inner qualities are mostly discovered by usage. Prestige buying seems to play a greater role than in the West. The price is not really part of the product; a discount is a psychological matter rather than an economic advantage. Thriftiness still characterizes the private life of the Japanese; it has little to do with industrial purchasing where expansion overshadows everything else.

The fact that purchasing may be "localized" in a purchasing department does not mean that it is actually performed there. Being a function of the whole, purchasing results easily in a certain rivalry among departments that has nothing to do with the intrinsic qualities of the product, but may well affect its price. This infighting puts the foreign marketer at a disadvantage unless he is already considered as a true insider. The foreign firm suffers from a great handicap if its Japanese representatives are not given enough leeway in negotiating specifications, price, delivery time, and the like, all aspects that in the in-fighting situation may help in adjusting conflicting opinions. On the other hand, practices are changing, as seen in the way business contracts are looked upon.

> "Japanese companies now are tending to prepare more forms with detailed clauses . . . [Out of ten persons, each with different companies] seven persons . . . explained the recent trend as a result of international contracts, which usually contain numerous clauses. Three others . . . said that they were merely following the fashion. . . . When domestic contracts are made for eventual import or export, contracts with foreign companies are sometimes attached, and many of their terms are made applicable to the domestic contracts. In this way, the companies would be free of criticism that they are imposing detailed clauses on their business partners."[13]

At the consumer level the manifestations of change are most obvious. Nonetheless, it seems safer to assume that the customer in tomorrow's Tokyo will not react as the customer in tomorrow's London or New York; the assimilation capacity of the Japanese is not a recent phenomenon: the acceptance of western technology seems to follow a pattern identical to the acceptance of Chinese civilization fifteen centuries ago.

The first concern of the marketer will be to determine the purchasing power of the population. For centuries a characteristic of most Asian populations has been the large gap between a small minority of very rich and the overwhelming majority of very poor; Japan is once more an exception: practically the total population is middle class. This makes for a very integrated consumer market and one where likes and dislikes take greater proportions at rapidly accumulating speed, compounded by the postwar development of the *danchi* ('apartment housing'), where several hundreds of house-

---

[13] Sawada, *op. cit.*, pp. 199–200 and 201.

holds conglomerate in brand-new market units. The middle-class mentality is strikingly manifested in the amazing rate of personal savings that recently increased to 20%. (Let it be said that this is contrary to the prediction of even the best among the Japanese economists.) Though such savings are "personal", their social merit should not be credited to the "individual". The feat is part of the fabric of Japan's industrial society through deferred wage payments, a very sophisticated collection system, and the network of interpersonal relations.

At all levels change is the rule, but let it be remembered that in Japan there is no real gap between tradition and change; the tradition is to change. Marketing is then like surfing: waves keep coming, but the surfer can ride only one at a time. To keep on top of the wave, some simple rules must be observed; they are universal, but should be given a special urgency in Japan because of the extraordinary rapidity of growth and change.[14]

1) Information about the market should be gathered on a continuous basis in order to reflect the continuous change; a common error is to rely on the latest data for decision; but before the decision comes to execution, "later" data are already available. Time series have more than a historical value; they should communicate a feel for the evolution always taking place.

2) The tentative picture of the market and the market environment should be open to question at any time. The foreign marketer will do this conceptually; his Japanese staff will do it rather by intuition. This easily results in a communication gap to be aware of.

3) The best marketing experiences of the home office should be made available to (not imposed on) our man in Japan. In their light he should review on a continuous basis any

14 The writer thanks Dr. Herbert Glazer for pointing out this need.

and all market decisions and strategies checked by an elaborate feedback system.

Some foreign marketers have been living in Japan for a decade or more, and several of them are quite successful. Does it mean that they are now Japanese? Not at all! One may spend a lifetime in Japan; he will still be considered a *gaijin* ('foreigner'), even if he acquires Japanese citizenship and speaks the language fluently. No foreigner ever becomes a Japanese. But these foreigners have developed an empathy for the people and the environment that enriches them. Dislike or hatred are mostly rooted in ignorance; because the "foreigners" are cognizant about Japan, they do not always like all they see, but they love and enjoy the challenge of Japan.

By the way, what happened to the products they represented? Many were assimilated and have been improved upon by Japanese competitors.

CHAPTER TWO

Your Presence in Japan

EUGENE H. LEE

Non-corporate presence: direct sales; the representative: an agent, a man in Japan—Corporate presence: the branch office; the subsidiary; joint-venture company—Trademarks

THIS chapter is concerned with the preparations advisable for foreign marketing in Japan, especially with the choice and establishment of a proper format. Even after several years of liberalization programs, the Japanese government still exercises controls that are of continuing importance to foreign firms in structuring their marketing activities. But differences in culture and tradition remain the most formidable barriers to foreigners in the country.

Organizing for marketing in Japan involves a careful balancing of many factors. Most important among them is the evaluation of how a firm actually wants to do business. Obviously a relatively small manufacturing company faces a completely different range of problems from those of a global industrial giant, and each must tailor its means for entering Japan to its individual strengths and weaknesses. Once the firm has decided upon its means, its project must undergo the test of Japanese government policies concerning foreign investment. In other words, how will the Japanese government allow a foreign company to do business in Japan? As will be seen later, the answer to this question is not always obvious; sometimes the only way to obtain a clear answer is to submit a specific plan to the government for formal decision. Regardless of ambiguities, the policies of the Japanese government cannot be ignored, for they play a vital role in the formulation of marketing strategies in the country.[1]

Non-corporate presence

DIRECT SALES

PROFESSOR Alfred F. Conard in an article on organizing for business in the Common Market compares the activities of many companies interested in doing business abroad to those of a timid bather preparing for a swim.[2] The bather may throw pebbles from the shore, dip his toes, wade, swim with his head out or dive into the water. In Japan, as in other countries, each stage of entry involves exposure to greater risks. We will try to approach in stages the problem of entry into Japan much like the bather inching his way into the water, indicating as we go some of the risks which have been charted through the experiences of previous bathers.

As we begin figuratively testing the water to see if it is suitable for swimming, the first tangible step that can be taken is to sell directly to Japan. Probably, in this simplest way, sales are typically made directly to a Japanese trading firm which then proceeds to distribute and market throughout Japan. For many companies this approach offers the most practical way to crack the Japanese market. Its simplicity is one of its greatest advantages, for it largely

---

[1] For general comments relating Japanese government policy to strategies for doing business in Japan, see James C. Abegglen (ed.), *Business Strategies for Japan*, Tokyo: Sophia University, 1970.

[2] Alfred F. Conard, "Organizing For Business", in Eric Stain and Thomas L. Nicholson (eds.), *American Enterprise in the European Common Market: A Legal Profile*, Vol. 2, Ann Arbor: The University of Michigan Law School, 1960, p. 1.

avoids complicated issues of foreign law and differences in business customs. If the foreign company has little or no business experience in Japan, direct sales can be an effective way to test the demand in the market and learn something about doing business in Japan without investing large sums of money. In addition, the need for government approval is minimized, and consequently little concerning the foreign company's business is disclosed to the government. If the sales are properly arranged, the company may avoid liability for Japanese tax and thus be concerned only with the tax requirements of its home country. In short, in most respects it is as if a line were drawn across the ocean. As long as the foreign business stays on its own side of the line, its marketing through trading companies which then sell to Japanese distributors is a relatively simple procedure.

A great many companies are not satisfied, however, with doing business from the outside. Direct sales often are not the best way to maximize business opportunities. After a product is manufactured abroad and imported to Japan it may no longer be competitive because of the expenses involved in foreign labor costs, transportation, and customs duties. More specifically related to marketing problems, the Japanese trading company which buys foreign products abroad may also deal in competitive goods (often manufactured by a sister company) and not appear to be aggressive enough in promoting sales. More simply, the problems involved in adequately explaining a product, especially a technical one, of handling installation, or of rendering after-sales service are such that on-the-spot representation may be necessary. For this reason many companies choose to ignore the safe line drawn across the ocean and become more deeply involved in Japan. This decision may have many consequences, the most important of which is that the company voluntarily places itself in the context of Japanese business as a whole and must swiftly learn to operate, or perhaps just to survive, in an environment that often bears little resemblance to the one at home.

THE REPRESENTATIVE

PLACING a representative in Japan is a relatively minimal method of entry. There are many ways of structuring and deploying this general form of organization for marketing. The representative could be an employee of the home company or, if the need for representation is only slight or non-technical, an agent might be hired instead of a regular employee. The agency could be structured in terms of a distributorship or franchise, or in terms of one of the specific types of agencies provided under Japanese law. If the need is merely for representation rather than for actual participation in marketing activities, the agent or employee could limit his activities to liaison and thus lessen the company's exposure to Japanese legal requirements.

1. *Agent*

Several different types of agents are provided for under Japanese law.[3] Although it is not necessary here to analyze the various types from a legal point of view, how the agent can be of practical usefulness to the foreign company's marketing program merits attention.

If the agent's independent posture is maintained he can engage in a wide scope of activities in Japan on his own account without involving the foreign company itself internally in Japan. One of the typical ways that he can be used is as a distributor of the foreign company's products. In essence, the distributor buys from the supplier and resells the same goods on his own account. A company can set up an entire network of distributors in Japan and still remain safely on the far side of the mid-ocean line as long as the

---

[3] Examples are the broker, described in Art. 543 *et seq.* of the Commercial Code of Japan (hereinafter called Commercial Code); the commission agent, Art. 551; the commercial agent, Art. 46; the forwarding agent, Art. 559; and the warehouseman, Art. 597.

relationship between the foreign company and the distributors is carefully structured in accordance with Japanese legal concepts.

Depending upon the commodities to be handled, granting franchises in Japan may also be an effective means of entering Japan. In the franchise relationship, use of the name of the foreign company and application of certain techniques concerning preparation and marketing of certain products are the primary benefits gained by the franchise holder in Japan. A typical example of the use of franchises is the restaurant chain which authorizes use of its name in the preparation and sale of its distinctive line of food products. The foreign food chain's main concern is protection of the value of its name through quality control and marketing techniques, and thus its investment in Japan and exposure to Japanese law are rather minimal.

Agreements establishing the basic relationship with either distributors or franchise holders usually must be submitted to the Japanese government for approval under the Foreign Exchange and Foreign Trade Control Law.[4] In general, approvals are not especially difficult to obtain for these types of agreements as long as the specific provisions are found to be fair. This means that some types of restrictions which the foreign company might prefer to place in an agreement with its distributor or franchise holder may need to be tempered to suit a particular situation, but that the basic relationship should be attainable except where the commodities in question are subject to special restriction under Japanese law.

---

[4] For instance, see *Gaikoku kawase oyobi bōeki kanrihō* (Foreign Exchange and Foreign Trade Control Law), Art. 27 (Law No. 228, 1949, as amended 1964), in 5 EHS No. 5010 (hereinafter cited FECA), and *Gaikoku kawase kanrirei* (Cabinet order concerning control of foreign exchange), Art. II (Cabinet Order No. 203, 1950), in 5 EHS No. 5030. For examples of how the FECA and the Cabinet Order are applied, see Teruo Doi, "The Validity of Contracts Made in Violation of the Forum's Exchange Controls", in *Law in Japan: An Annual*, Vol. 2, Tokyo: Japanese-American Society for Legal Studies, 1968, p. 180.

2. *A Man in Japan*

If what is needed in Japan is mere representation that falls short of transacting business, an agent or an employee of the home company stationed in Japan may be the best arrangement. For many companies, it is more desirable to station one of their own employees in Japan than to find an indigenous agent. As one who is familiar with the business of the company, an experienced employee may not only be more useful in furthering the business in Japan, but may also be able to communicate more effectively with the home office. Moreover, his position as a full-time employee enables him to give his full attention to the company's problems without being drawn into conflict-of-interest situations that sometimes befall agents.

When a company decides to place a man in Japan, however, certain concomitant problems arise, not the least of which is simply getting the representative there. The first hurdle is to secure the proper visa.[5] If the employee is to work in Japan, only two of the sixteen different types of Japanese visas are relevant. They are the commercial visa (4–1–5) and the short-term commercial visa (4–1–16–1). Under the former, residence for commercial purposes is allowed for periods up to three years. Under the latter, one can stay in Japan for commercial purposes for up to 180 days at a time. Renewals of both categories are possible, but involve additional screening and presentation of justifications in support of renewal.

Relatively easy to obtain, the short-term commercial visa is usually issued immediately by a local Japanese consulate after good commercial reasons for a stay in Japan are demonstrated. The three-year commercial visa is more difficult and time-consuming

---

[5] For detailed information on visas, see G. Grega, "A Review of Visa Regulations", in *The Journal of the American Chamber of Commerce in Japan,* May 1966, p. 42.

to obtain and requires a statement of the applicant's proposed activities in Japan. Generally, because the decision on the granting of this visa is made in Japan rather than by a local consulate, several weeks or even months may be needed for processing. Generally also, the application for the three-year commercial visa must be supported with a showing that the purpose of residence in Japan is: (1) to enable the applicant to operate his own business, (2) to enable him to be employed by a Japanese company, or (3) to enable him to be employed by a Japanese branch of a foreign company.

In many cases these requirements for obtaining a long-term commercial visa may preclude its use by the representative of a company that would like to have a man on the scene but does not wish to announce its presence (to the government or to competitors) by registering a branch in Japan. Thus the short-term visa is sometimes preferable since it involves less demonstration of a presence in Japan and does not imply a continuing need for the foreign company to maintain a resident employee.

Visa information and applications can be obtained at any Japanese consulate or embassy. Such information is usually consistent, but because problems seem sometimes to vary between consulates, the nearest consulate should be consulted for specific advice.

Once the representative is finally located in Japan, the next problem that immediately arises is the scope of the activities he can properly effect on behalf of the home company—a problem that will continue to engage both the representative and his superiors at home for the duration of his presence in Japan. The main restriction on his activities as an individual representative will be that he cannot "transact business" on behalf of the home company. This restriction has two primary sources. One is that under the Japanese Commercial Code a foreign company must register a branch office if it is engaging in "commercial transactions as a continuing business in Japan" (Art. 473). The other reason is that he may be held for tax purposes to be a permanent establishment of the home company, thus bringing other Japanese income of the company into the ambit of Japanese taxation.

Given what the employee cannot do in Japan, what is there left that he can do? In the area of marketing, there are many services manageable by a representative that do not involve commercial transactions or connection with a permanent establishment in Japan—for example, such things as market research, general promotion, and liaison with the home office and with potential or established customers in Japan. These sorts of services could be most valuable to a company trying to extend its market in Japan and still allow the company to stay as far removed as possible from exposure to Japanese legal and governmental controls.

The representative could stay in Japan on an indefinite basis or could limit his stay to the duration of a specific project. For instance, assume that a foreign company would like to initiate a promotion campaign for a specific product and feels that it therefore needs to have at least one employee present in Japan to help in coordinating its efforts. From its office abroad it could make all its advertising arrangements with Japanese advertising firms and then send one or more employees to Japan to conduct market surveys and collect information at the same time that its advertising campaign is being held. As long as a representative's activities were limited to liaison, there would be no need to file a branch report. Many personnel of foreign companies come to Japan on an occasional basis to oversee promotional programs. Should their activities in Japan become too extensive, however, the danger always exists that the government might suspect that they are abusing their exceptional status and move to restrict the liaison exemption in some degree.

A decision to employ a liaison representative for Japan who does not engage in commercial transactions may lead to a variety of problems. One is that he may be jointly and severally liable with the home company if he actually conducts business transactions in Japan (Commercial Code Art. 481.2). Additionally, lacking an office registered in Japan, he may have to suffer both personal and professional inconvenience. For instance, he may find it difficult to rent or buy certain kinds of property in the name of the company (e.g. land, an automobile, etc.). Furthermore, he may have to maintain all corporate bank accounts in his own name since it may be impossible to establish a bank account in the name of a non-registered company. If he needs to handle import or export procedures in the name of the company he may face additional problems. Finally, it must be remembered that personal and group identities are matters of paramount importance in Japan. The name that appears on the door of an office and the representation that appears on a name card are often key elements in the effectiveness of personnel operating in Japan, where status and prestige are of extreme importance to business associations.[6]

Corporate presence

THE BRANCH OFFICE

IF the difficulties encountered by representatives in Japan seem to outweigh the advantages of maintaining a posture of minimal presence, a decision may be made to register a branch office. Such a registration can be made in situations where it is not legally required. In other words, the branch office's activities could be limited to liaison services designed generally to further the sales of products in Japan through market research, promotion, liaison, and the like, but not to involve participation in commercial transactions. This would mean that the home company would have a formal presence in Japan but, because the branch activities fall within the limits of exemption for liaison, there would be no

---

[6] For an exceptional analysis of Japanese society and specific comments on this point, see Chie Nakane, *Japanese Society*, Berkeley: University of California, 1970, p. 92.

permanent establishment there. As a safeguard for this last condition, it is often preferable for a branch office to be registered by a related company that has little or no connection with Japan and for the branch to collect a fee for the services it performs on behalf of other companies.

Registration of a branch involves two formalities. Under the foreign-exchange control laws, an advance report of the branch's proposed business must be filed with the government. If the government approves the report, the branch is formally registered under the Commercial Code. The time required for processing the report may vary with the circumstances. If all goes well, the process usually takes approximately one month. If problems develop during the course of governmental review, registration can be delayed indefinitely. However, if the branch is to engage merely in liaison, the approval process generally progresses smoothly.

Although the simple act of registration of a branch does not give rise to liability for Japanese tax, it does publicize the presence of the foreign company in Japan and may therefore draw the attention of tax officials and lead to a tax audit.

Registration of a branch often proves especially useful if the employees of the home company are to be present in Japan for an extended period of time. Not only does it provide status and recognition and facilitate solution of basic problems of existence such as the induction of funds and acquisition of office space, but it also seems to legitimize the activities of the foreign company in Japan by giving the impression that it has nothing to hide.

The liaison branch office usually is reimbursed by its home office for its expenses and earns no income in Japan. If it properly limits its activities, it may successfully avoid becoming a permanent establishment of one of its related companies abroad, and thus none of the members of the overseas corporate family will be subject to Japanese taxation due to the presence or activities of the Japan branch. Tax officials in Japan seem to have come to the view that the presence of a branch office of a foreign firm obviously means that the Japan branch is valuable to the overall activities of the company or it would not exist. Therefore, the official reasoning is that the branch office should have some tax liability in Japan regardless of whether it is productive of income or not. This attitude has usually been placated if the branch reports an income based on a modest percentage of its expenses. Since this type of income calculation bears no resemblance to the value to the home company of having a branch office in Japan, it is merely token payment to give Japan some benefit for permitting the foreign presence.

The basic problem for the foreign company may be whether the support activities which a representative or a liaison branch office may offer are really adequate to attain its marketing objectives in Japan. Market research, customer contact, and feedback to the home company on a variety of problems ranging from what Japanese eat for breakfast to what competitors are up to are valuable, but may fall short of satisfying the company's business needs. It is at this point that the most difficult decisions must be made, for activities beyond mere liaison terminate, as it were, the swimmer's gradual inching into the water and amount to a head-first plunge.

Since a report must usually be filed with the government before a branch of a foreign company can be established, the government will examine all aspects of the branch's activity from the point of view of official controls on the use of foreign capital in Japan. The control standards of the Japanese government have been developed through law, regulations, and precedents and are designed to restrict the intrusion into the Japanese market of foreign firms whose activities may create difficulties within that market.[7]

[7] For an interesting comparison of views concerning the legality of Japan's restriction of foreign investment, see articles by Professors Shinichirō Michida and Yasuhiro Fujita which have been published in English. For legal strategies for challenging the*

In the case of marketing in Japan there are several observations that might be made which are relevant to apparent governmental attitudes and standards. First, as a general rule, the establishment of a branch of a foreign company which is to market actively in Japan (i.e., buy from related firms outside Japan and sell within Japan) is generally considered permissible if the commodities at issue do not involve especially sensitive areas of the Japanese economy. In other words, if the commodities to be sold by the Japanese branch are ICs, transistors, or aero-space products, adverse government opinion would be the rule rather than the exception. In addition, a firm that wishes to sell through its branch in Japan must probably deal in goods imported into Japan rather than in goods manufactured in Japan. There are a great many trading firms in Japan which do a very good job of distributing Japanese products throughout the country, and the prevailing official attitude towards them seems to be that foreign capital is simply not needed as a stimulant in the Japanese market itself.

In addition to the types of commodities to be sold by the Japanese branch, both the amount of capital to be used for its initial operating funds and the means whereby it is to be paid are critical points. Excessive amounts of capital could be used to upset the balance of the Japanese economy, or at least the balance within a particular industry, and so the specific amounts brought into Japan need to be officially reported, justified, and approved.

Once the marketing branch has been established, its future

---

*Japanese restrictions, see Shinichirō Michida, "Capital Liberalization As a Treaty Question and Offensive and Defensive Strategies Concerning Foreign Capital", in *Law In Japan: An Annual*, Vol. 2, Tokyo: Japanese-American Society for Legal Studies, 1968, p. 1. While not necessarily contending that the Japanese government's liberalization policies are wise, Professor Fujita defends their legality under Japan's treaty commitments in response to Professor Michida's article. See Yasuhiro Fujita, "Does Japan's Restriction on Foreign Capital Entries Violate Her Treaties—in Response to Michida Article", in *Law In Japan: An Annual*, Vol. 3, Tokyo: Japanese-American Society For Legal Studies, 1960, p. 162. Also see Herbert Glazer, *The International Businessman in Japan*, Tokyo: Sophia University, 1968, p. 28 ff.

activities must be limited to those set forth in the report approved by the government. If new activities are desired, a new report to amend the branch's activities must be filed. This extension requires in effect a new application and a duplication of all the same information and justifications necessary at the outset. Since the branch would be actively engaging in business in Japan, it could then show a profit upon which Japanese tax could be based. In addition, if the branch should constitute the permanent establishment in Japan of any other entity, that other entity would have to pay Japanese tax on all of its income attributable to Japan. Thus, preferably, the branch should be registered by a member of the corporate family which does not have non-taxed income from Japanese sources. In organizing the branch's business activities it is important to make sure that transactions between the branch and related companies are also considered from the tax viewpoint. Otherwise, Japanese tax officials might interpret any unusual dealing arrangements as evidence that the branch is not really independent but acting on behalf of another company. The result could be the finding of a permanent establishment in Japan.

THE SUBSIDIARY

ANOTHER way to use the corporate form to secure insulation from the reach of Japanese law is to form a Japanese company which will engage in business in Japan on its own behalf. A great deal of publicity has been given in recent years to the difficulties in securing governmental approval for the establishment in Japan of wholly owned subsidiaries of foreign firms. Indeed, the difficulties in this type of establishment still exist in spite of four rounds of government liberalization. Although in the eyes of impatient foreign businessmen the progress seems slight, there seems to be no doubt that attitudes have been changing gradually in the direction of liberalization of capital investments from abroad. There are still, however, many sensitive industries in which investments by foreigners cannot be made in any sizeable amount and in which any investment is always subject to government approval and conditions.

Marketing especially is an area where formation of a wholly owned subsidiary is not beyond the realm of possibility. There are several marketing firms operating in Japan on this basis at the present time; in fact, one of the initial breakthroughs in the government's resistance against the establishment of subsidiaries of foreign firms in Japan came several years ago in the form of a subsidiary to market the goods of related companies in Japan. The considerations for securing governmental approval of a marketing subsidiary in Japan are similar to those mentioned previously for the registration of a branch office. In short, the commodities in which the subsidiary is to deal must be ones not considered especially sensitive and must have been imported into Japan rather than purchased in Japan for resale in the same market. The amount of the investment will be carefully controlled and amounts invested will need to be carefully justified.

The establishment of a subsidiary company in Japan is subject to prior approval of the Japanese government. Through a formal application submitted to the Bank of Japan, all particulars of the investment are revealed to the Foreign Investment Council and concerned government ministries. The articles of incorporation, related agreements (if any), and an explanatory statement detailing how the investment will benefit the Japanese economy are attached.

If the investment is covered by the announced liberalization program and does not include features worrisome to the officials, the screening may be completed within one month under the so-called "automatic approval" system. Quite likely, however, specific questions will arise, and negotiations with officials will proceed on a case by case basis. Timing of an approval under these circumstances is nearly impossible to predict. Also, approval may be conditioned on certain restrictions voluntarily assumed by the applicant.

Once the approval is obtained, the shares must be subscribed and paid and the company must be formally registered. These are routine formalities once the basic approval has been obtained.

Since the subsidiary is a separate corporate entity, it will be subject to Japanese tax on its earnings in the same way as any other Japanese company. The subsidiary would engage in the importation and sale of goods made by a related company, and the margin of profit from such transactions would constitute its gross income. The pricing of goods between the related companies would have to be fair and reasonable to support the subsidiary's stance as a separate and independent entity. The capital structure and the activities of the subsidiary should be substantial to support this claim further. If, on the other hand, it were apparent that the parent company or a related company was really conducting the business rather than the subsidiary, there is a danger that tax officials might ignore the corporate form and claim that it is really the parent company that is conducting the business rather than the subsidiary. This means that the need for fair dealing between related parties cannot be stressed too strongly.

JOINT-VENTURE COMPANY

IN principle, the procedures necessary to obtain approval and register a joint-venture company are the same as for a wholly owned subsidiary. However, the presence of a Japanese partner can be very helpful in securing smooth government processing. Major Japanese companies generally have good working relations with various government officials and may be in a position to block opposition to the investment proposal from other members of the industry.[8]

[8] For general background concerning various aspects of the joint-venture company in Japan, see Robert J. Ballon and Eugene H. Lee (eds.), *Foreign Investment and Japan*, Tokyo: Kodansha-Sophia, 1972; Robert J. Ballon, *Joint Ventures in Japan* (pamphlet in the series *Business in Japan: Guidelines for Exporters*, London: Japan Air Lines' European Regional Office, 1972.)

Joint-venture companies have been used primarily for manufacturing in industries not yet open to investment on a 100% basis. The joint-venture formula ensures that protected industries will not fall under the control of foreign concerns. In the screening of joint-venture applications, care is normally taken to assure that there are no features of the proposal whereby the foreign party can secure a greater degree of corporate control than his shareholding ratio warrants. Consequently, it is difficult to screen the Japanese partner from access to technology to be used by the joint-venture company or to obtain enforceable commitments to acquire a higher shareholding interest at some future date. The Japanese partner must normally be fully represented in management, a contingency which often means a Japanese president.

While joint ventures for marketing only are unusual, manufacturing joint ventures are actively engaged in marketing their products in Japan. In some cases this seems to have been a successful arrangement. Marketing techniques in Japan differ so radically from those of the West that the joint-venture partner can contribute enormously valuable expertise.

The issue of corporate control is always one of the most delicate in joint ventures. Each party would often prefer to exercise control independently and yet finds that his partner has a "veto power" over his proposals. For the foreign company, this veto power often represents the outer limit of its actual control since a largely Japanese-staffed operation seems to generate its own momentum. This veto position can be strengthened by ensuring that the articles of incorporation offer adequate protection by stipulations for adequate quorums and voting majorities at meetings of shareholders and directors. In fact, through such stipulations veto power can be maintained even though the party owns less than 50% of the shares.

Trademarks

TRADEMARKS are of course visible signs of the presence of marketing companies. Japanese trademark law and practice pretty much parallel their counterparts in the West. Trademarks are registered through formal application to the Japanese Patent Office, which in due course appraises their registrability in Japan. Early registration of trademarks is usually advisable since there have been instances where well-known foreign marks have been previously registered by parties in Japan who then try to "sell" the mark to the foreign companies concerned. Theoretically it is possible for a registered trademark to be cancelled because of "non-use"; however, this technique has been used very seldom and does not normally seem to constitute a serious danger.

The trademark can be used by the owner or can be licensed to third parties, or both. Both exclusive licenses and non-exclusive licenses are commonly granted. It is possible also to register specific license rights with the Patent Office, but such registration is optional and foreign licensors often prefer not to exercise this option since the registration may vest the licensee with certain rights under Japanese law that may not have been intended and could provide the licensee with an additional means of contesting a termination of the license agreement by the licensor.

Trademark licenses can be royalty bearing, but royalty amounts have generally been small.

A trademark license is formally submitted for government validation through an application to the Bank of Japan and, as an international contract, is submitted to the Fair Trade Commission for screening.

The choice of a type of presence for Japan does not have to be a permanent one. Japan is flexible and undergoing rapid change and foreign companies marketing there need to be able to adapt quickly to the circumstances. In view of current proposals for further liberalization of capital investment, companies may some-day have wider options for structuring their presence. This, coupled with Japan's rapid growth, counsels the need to keep options open.

Regardless of the type of presence in Japan, the role that government plays in business will remain a factor of importance, and this role is unlikely to change fundamentally in the near future. This, too, is a final consideration and challenge for establishing and maintaining a successful presence in Japan!

CHAPTER THREE

Antimonopoly Regulation
of Marketing

MITSUO MATSUSHITA AND EUGENE H. LEE

Pricing activities: horizontal price fixing; vertical price
fixing and resale price maintenance; price discrimination
and dumping—Channels of distribution: use of trade-
marks; contractual restrictions—Advertisement and sale
with premiums—Appendices

IN Japan terms such as "orderly marketing" and "avoidance of
excessive competition" are frequently mouthed by businessman
and government official alike. The westerner soon begins to suspect that the dynamics of antimonopoly regulation in Japan differ
radically from those in the West. In part this may be true, but,
as will be seen below, antimonopoly regulation is also actively used
to protect consumers from abuse of monopolistic power.

In general, the Antimonopoly Act (hereinafter called the "Act")
stipulates three major types of regulation: (1) prohibition of private
monopoly, (2) prohibition of unreasonable restraints on trade, and
(3) prohibition of unfair business practices. The area of unfair
business practices is most relevant to legal problems relating to
marketing in Japan. Unfair business practices are set forth in
Section 2(7) of the Act. (Appendix 1.) In addition to the provisions
contained in the Act, the Fair Trade Commission is empowered to

designate, as unfair trade practices, specific acts falling under any one of the categories specified in the Act which tend to impede fair competition. Pursuant to this authorization, the Fair Trade Commission issued its *General Designation of Unfair Business Practices*, which designates twelve kinds of activities as constituting unfair trade practices. (Appendix 2.) Among them are included boycotts and other refusals to deal, various kinds of discrimination regarding the terms of transactions, price discrimination, selling at unduly high or low prices, inducing or coercing competitors or customers to deal with oneself, exclusive dealing arrangements, tying arrangements, and the misuse of a dominant position over other parties. A series of notifications have also been issued by the Fair Trade Commission designating specific unfair business practices for specific industries.[1]

Not all of the important antimonopoly issues related to marketing are included in the unfair business practices designated by the Fair Trade Commission. For instance, one important exception is the problem of price agreements among competitors. This means that the discussion must be extended beyond the scope of unfair trade practices to include other aspects of antimonopoly law as well. Individual problems will be considered in three separate sections: (1) problems relating to pricing activities, (2) problems relating to channels of distribution, such as exclusive dealing arrangements, and (3) problems relating to advertising and premiums.

---

[1] Examples include "Specific Unfair Trade Practices in the Newspaper Industry," *Fair Trade Commission Notification No. 3* (1955); "Specific Unfair Trade Practices in the Textbook Industry," *Fair Trade Commission Notification No. 5* (1956); "Specific Unfair Trade Practices in the *Miso* Industry," *Fair Trade Commission Notification No. 13* (1953); "Specific Unfair Trade Practices in the Soy Sauce Industry," *Fair Trade Commission Notification No. 12* (1953); "Fair Trade Practices in the Marine Transport Industry," *Fair Trade Commission Notification No. 17* (1959); "Specific Unfair Trade Practices in the Animal and Whale Meat, Etc., Canning Industry," *Fair Trade Commission Notification No. 1* (1961).

Chapter Three. Antimonopoly Regulation of Marketing

Pricing activities

THREE major points fall under this heading: horizontal price fixing, vertical price fixing, and price discrimination.

HORIZONTAL PRICE FIXING

HORIZONTAL price fixing among competitors is prohibited under the Act. This prohibition does not, however, make horizontal price fixing a *per se* illegality as it is under American antitrust laws. Instead, under Japanese law, horizontal price fixing is illegal when such price-fixing agreement substantially restrains competition in a particular field of trade. The relevant provision of the Act is Section 2(6) which reads as follows:

> "The term 'unreasonable restraint of trade' as used in this Act shall mean such business activities, by which entrepreneurs by contract, agreement, or any other concerted activities mutually restrict or conduct their business activities in such a manner as to fix, maintain, or enhance prices; or to limit production, technology, products, facilities, or customers or suppliers, thereby causing, contrary to the public interest, a substantial restraint of competition in any particular field of trade."

According to this provision, a price-fixing agreement among competitors is to be held illegal if it causes a substantial restraint of competition in any particular field of trade. The problem is the meaning of "substantial restraint of competition". Every agreement concerning price is a restraint on competition to some extent; however, a restraint must be "substantial", which is a difficult requirement to interpret in the absence of a standard that can be applied to all situations. From the court decisions which have been decided in this context, we can derive the general rule that substantial restraint of competition refers to situations where effective competition can no longer be expected.[2] This occurs most frequently where the parties participating in such price-fixing arrangements hold overwhelming power over the market. Under this approach, the parties would almost have to be in control of the market to be in violation of Section 2(6). This element of market domination or control is measured by various factors, such as the market share, the number of enterprises in the market, and the strength of competitors not participating in the agreement. In most cases of previous interpretation made by the courts and the Fair Trade Commission the parties participating in the illegal agreement had a large market share, such as 50% or more.[3] There may be exceptions to this approach where a finding of illegality will not result. One example might be where the market in question is small and all competitors are unreasonably weak.

Mere price leadership can be distinguished from price fixing since there are only price leaders and followers. If the price leader sets his price and others in the same business follow, there is no element of conspiracy or agreement and thus no illegality. This may be what was involved in the recent rise in the price of beer throughout Japan which attracted the attention of the Fair Trade Commission, the Economic Planning Agency, and the public at large. Even though price leadership and the so-called administered price are not illegal as such, the circumstances surrounding a unilateral price rise may result in a finding of illegality. An example is *Noda*

---

[2] Tōhō Kabushiki Kaisha v. FTC, *4 Kōsai Minshu* (1951), p. 479; Tōhō Kabushiki Kaisha v. FTC, *6 Kōsai Minshu* (1953), p. 868; Nihon Sekiyu Kabushiki Kaisha *et al.* v. FTC, *7 Gyōsei Reishū* (1956), p. 2849.

[3] For instance, in the case of *Tōhō Kabushiki Kaisha v. FTC (supra)*, the parties accused of being involved in an illegal agreement had control of 57.9% of the market for the exhibition of motion pictures. In *Nihon Sekiyu Kabushiki Kaisha v. FTC (supra)*, parties engaged in the sale of petroleum products fixed prices. Here the parties controlled over 90% of the market. In addition to market share, it must be pointed out that the number of enterprises involved and the strength of competitors also should be taken into consideration.

Shōyu Kabushiki Kaisha v. FTC[4] in which the Fair Trade Commission issued a cease-and-desist order against the maker of the popular high-grade KIKKOMAN soy sauce. Noda, which had nearly 40% of the high-grade soy sauce market in Japan, raised its price and coerced all dealers by pressure and threat to sell at the new price. This action forced competitors to raise their prices in order to avoid damage to the reputation for superior quality enjoyed by their products. In using its power to control the price of its own product, Noda was said to have controlled also the business activities of other entrepreneurs, thereby causing, contrary to the public interest, a substantial restraint of competition in a particular field of trade—in other words, private monopolization.

An agreement between competitors can be implied by circumstantial evidence in the absence of a written agreement. An example is *FTC v. Yuasa Timber Co.*[5] in which an implied agreement was construed from the fact that representatives from various competing timber companies had met for dinner on several occasions, discussed prices, and applauded speakers who expressed approval of prices of a certain level. The defendant company argued that there was no agreement between the companies, but the Fair Trade Commission felt that the facts were adequate to hold that there was an implied agreement. Thus, in oligopolistic situations where price leadership exists, implied agreements can be established more easily and will be held to be illegal if the Fair Trade Commission can acquire enough evidence that an agreement may have been made.

In this connection, agreements which purport not to fix prices but rather to exchange information also should be briefly mentioned. If the information relates to the pricing of competitors, the

---

[4] Noda Shōyu Kabushiki Kaisha v. FTC, *10 Kōsai Minshu* (1955), p. 743.

[5] FTC v. Yuasa Timber Co., *1 Kōsei Torihiki Iinkai Shinketsushū* (hereinafter called "*FTC Decision Reports*") (1949), p. 62. For a similar case, see Nihon Sekiyu Kabushiki Kaisha v. FTC, *supra* note 2.

exchange is not necessarily beyond the sweep of the Act and might be held to be a price-fixing agreement in substance. The Fair Trade Commission has decided a case which illustrates this point. In this case, a barber shop cooperative sent questionnaires to members soliciting their views on proper prices. On the surface this questionnaire was for research purposes, but the Fair Trade Commission held that it was in effect price direction imposed by a trade association on its members and was therefore illegal.[6]

VERTICAL PRICE FIXING AND RESALE PRICE MAINTENANCE

IN American antitrust law, the model for the Japanese law,[7] there seems to be no difference in the application of the antitrust laws regardless of whether the agreement to fix prices is vertical or horizontal. Both could be held to be a conspiracy to fix prices under the Sherman Act. In Japanese law, however, a distinction is made between horizontal price-fixing agreements and vertical price-fixing agreements and different rules are applied to each. Vertical price-fixing agreements, in this context agreements relating to resale price maintenance, are not considered to be a type of cartel, but are held to be an unreasonable business practice. On the other hand, in terms of the way the law seems to be applied, there must be a "substantial restraint of trade" to hold a horizontal price-fixing agreement illegal. Since resale price maintenance falls under Section 2(7) of the Act, to hold a resale price-maintenance agreement illegal, the agreement must have a tendency to impede fair competition. This presents differences in semantics. As discussed above, substantial restraint of competition often boils down to

---

[6] FTC v. Akitashi Chūō Riyōkumiai, *13 FTC Decision Reports* (1965), p. 55.

[7] See Y. Kanazawa, "The Regulation of Corporate Enterprise: The Law of Unfair Competition and the Control of Monopoly Power" in A. Von Mehren (ed.), *Law in Japan*, Cambridge: Harvard University Press, 1963, p. 485. On the historical background and economic effect of the Act, see E. M. Hadley, *Antitrust in Japan*, Princeton: Princeton University Press, 1970.

control of the market. Impediment of fair competition, however, covers situations where a tendency is found that a controlling power may be formed in the market. There is also a provision in the Act exempting resale price-maintenance contracts from the application of the law in certain situations (Section 24–2).

It is worthwhile to take a brief look at the situations where resale price maintenance is exempted from the application of the Act. First, the commodities must be ones that have been designated by the Fair Trade Commission. To qualify for such a designation, the commodities in question must have the following characteristics:

a) They must be for daily use by general consumers;
b) Free competition must exist with respect to the commodity; and
c) Uniform quality of the commodity must be easy to identify (Trademarked goods) (Section 24–2(2)).

So far, the Fair Trade Commission's designations have included soap, cosmetics, toothpaste, drugs, and cameras as exempted commodities. In spite of this fact, exemptions are not allowed if the resale price maintenance contract is likely to grossly injure the interests of general consumers or if such contract is made against the will of the producers. This exemption is limited to individual resale price-maintenance contracts; collective activities designed to maintain resale prices are not exempted.[8]

If a resale price-maintenance contract is made with respect to a commodity not having such a qualification, the agreement is held to constitute an unfair business practice. There are several cases where resale price-maintenance agreements have been held illegal, and this aspect of the Act has become more important recently because of the rise in consumer prices, which is said to be caused

[8] For details see H. Hasegawa, *Saihanbai Kakaku Iji Seido* ('Resale Price Maintenance System'), Tokyo: 1968.

in part by resale price-maintenance agreements.[9] Some pressure has been put on the Fair Trade Commission to examine whether the exemption for maintaining resale prices now enjoyed by several industries is actually necessary with a view to reducing the number of exempted commodities.

PRICE DISCRIMINATION AND DUMPING

PRICE discrimination and dumping are used here to refer to situations where an enterprise sells its commodities at very low prices and eliminates its competitors through such pricing policy. In this sense, price discrimination and dumping are similar. But, from the standpoint of the regulation set forth in the Act, these two areas are treated differently.

Price discrimination falls under item (4) of the *General Designation of Unfair Business Practices* and Section 2(7)(i) of the Act, and refers to situations where an enterprise maintains high prices in the areas where it has the power to control the market, but sells at low prices in areas where competition is keen. There have also been instances where price discrimination has been made not on a territorial basis, but on the basis of type of customer. Both of these

---

[9] FTC v. Kabushiki Kaisha Nakayama Taiyōdō, *2 FTC Decision Reports* (1951), p. 255; FTC v. Kaō Sekken Kabushiki Kaisha, *13 FTC Decision Reports* (1965), p. 14; FTC v. Kabushiki Kaisha Yakuruto Honsha, *Ibid.*, p. 72; FTC v. Meiji Shōji Kabushiki Kaisha, *15 FTC Decision Reports* (1966), p. 67; FTC v. Morinaga Shōji Kabukishi Kaisha, *Ibid.*, p. 84; FTC v. Wakōdō Kabushiki Kaisha, *Ibid.*, p. 98. Although all of these decisions have been decided by the FTC, some of them apparently are being appealed to the judiciary which will have the final word on the question of legality of resale price maintenance which apparently has been used widely in Japan, as illustrated by the *Meiji*, *Morinaga*, and *Wakōdō* cases. Since the margin of profit in the distribution of products is often very low in Japan, many distributors have found it necessary to rely on rebates from the manufacturer for the major portion of their profit. In view of the distributors' economic reliance on the rebates, some manufacturers have conditioned the rebate upon the degree to which the distributor maintains the manufacturer's resale prices. The FTC's view as expressed in the cases mentioned above is that this type of conditioned rebate is a form of coercion to enforce resale prices and constitutes an unfair business practice.

types of price discrimination are held illegal if they impede fair competition; that is to say, if they tend to drive competitors out of the market and thereby create a monopoly. The discrimination in price may be acceptable, however, if it is the result of differences in built-in variables such as freight costs and the volume of the purchase. Price discrimination may also be acceptable if it is for the purpose of meeting competition ("meeting" but not "beating"). Since this principle also applies to the customers who are the recipients of the commodities, the customers may also be held to be in violation of the Act. *FTC v. Hokkoku Shimbunsha*[10] is a case decided by the Tokyo High Court in the area of price discrimination which illustrates one of the principal situations where price discrimination becomes an impediment to fair competition. In this case the defendant newspaper company was located in Ishikawa Prefecture and had no real competition within its own prefecture. There was, however, another newspaper company which operated in neighboring Toyama Prefecture. The defendant started selling virtually the same newspaper printed for use in Ishikawa Prefecture in Toyama Prefecture in competition with the company already located there. However, the newspaper, sold in the area where the competitor made sales, was sold at a lower price than the same paper in areas where there was no competition. The competitor was not actually eliminated in this case, but the Fair Trade Commission found that there was a tendency to eliminate competition and asked the court for a temporary injunction to stop the discriminatory pricing practice. The FTC view is that such a practice may result in driving competitors from the market and creating a monopoly.

The Act also has provisions which regulate dumping [Section 2(7)(ii); *General Designation* Items (4), (5) and (10)]. If a violation of the Act is found, the Fair Trade Commission is authorized to issue a cease-and-desist order (Section 20). The jurisdiction of the

---

[10] FTC v. Hokkoku Shimbunsha, 5 *Gyōsei Reishū* (1957), p. 443.

Act is not clear and has been the subject of debate within Japan.[11] Generally, it appears that all or a part of the activity which is in violation of the Act must be carried out in Japan before the Act is relevant, which points out the ineffectiveness of the Act in dealing with acts of dumping which take place outside of Japan.

In addition to the coverage of the antimonopoly laws, the Customs Tariff Law provides for special duties to be applied to prevent dumping in Japan. (Appendix 3.) Under this law, anyone can file a complaint with the Japanese government alleging that the importation of goods into Japan or the resale of such goods within Japan has damaged or threatens to damage a Japanese industry or the establishment of a Japanese industry. If the government agrees with the complaint, it may authorize the customs officials to impose an additional special duty on the product in the amount of the difference between the fair dutiable value and the dumping price.

The General Agreement on Tariffs and Trade (GATT) also has provisions relevant to dumping. (Appendix 4.) Japan has ratified this treaty and these provisions should be available for use in combating dumping.

Channels of distribution

WHEN manufacturers want to establish channels of distribution, they often choose between entering agreements with distributors or retailers under which those distributors or retailers are bound to sell the manufacturer's commodities and granting franchises to distributors for specific areas. There is nothing inherently illegal in either of these two types of arrangements. However, it is possible to incorporate various restrictive conditions into such distributor agreements and these may sometimes be held illegal in Japan. The

---

[11] For a discussion of the jurisdiction of the Act and problems inherent in its interpretation, see M. Matsushita, "The Antimonopoly Act of Japan and International Transactions", in *The Japanese Annual of International Law,* No. 14 (1970), pp. 4 ff.

problem thus becomes one of evaluating what kinds of restrictive conditions are illegal in what kinds of situations. Only a few of the numerous problems in this area can be touched upon here.

Starting with the simplest type of example, when a manufacturer enters agreements with distributors under which he is to supply its commodities and the distributors are to sell such commodities, there is no illegality. However, if the distributors are further obligated to handle only the commodities of that manufacturer, a potentiality for a finding of illegality is created. Although these problems are rarely litigated, there are some decisions which say that exclusive distributorships are illegal.[12] The rationale for these decisions is that exclusive distributorships sometimes fall under Section 2(7) of the Act and constitute an unfair business practice. This kind of exclusive dealing arrangement is held illegal only if it impedes fair competition which involves a factual analysis of the business pattern. Under the decisions mentioned above, a finding of illegality has usually resulted where the manufacturer or the other enterprise imposing the exclusive relationship has been considerably stronger than the other party and where the manufacturer or other enterprises controlled many distributors through such agreements. A basic reason for this approach is that if powerful manufacturers or enterprises impose this type of exclusive distributorship on many distributors, the competitors of such manufacturers will be deprived of channels of distribution. It is difficult to evaluate how powerful the manufacturer or distributor must be for their arrangement to be held illegal, for illegality here can be considered only on a case-by-case basis.

---

12 For examples, see FTC v. Marukin Shōyu Kabushiki Kaisha, *1 FTC Decision Reports* (1950), p. 129; FTC v. Chūkyō Lion Hamigaki Kaisha, *4 FTC Decision Reports* (1953), p. 106; FTC v. Taishō Seiyaku Kabushiki Kaisha, *7 FTC Decision Reports* (1953), p. 99; Hokkaido Shimbunsha v. FTC, *15 Kōsai Minshu* (1955), p. 116. For a contrary result, see FTC v. Nihon Kōgaku Kabushiki Kaisha, *4 FTC Decision Reports* (1952), p. 46.

Marketing in Japan, Part I

A NEW development concerning the use of exclusive distributorships has appeared as a result of the 1971 yen revaluation. After the revaluation, it was expected that the prices of some imported products, especially liquor, cosmetics, and other consumer goods, would go down. However, the expected price reduction did not occur, and it was suspected that the sole agency system used in the importation of many foreign products was one cause.

Foreign producers often appoint domestic firms or foreign firms operating in Japan as sole distribution agents, granting them the exclusive license to sell under their registered trademarks in Japan. These sole agents register the right to exclusive use of the trademarks with the Patent Office and under Section 21 of the Tariff Act of Japan can prohibit importation of any articles which infringe the domestic trademark right by reporting to Customs the intention to block importation of the articles. Afterwards, Customs officials refuse entry of articles bearing the same trademark. In this way sole agents have been able effectively to prevent parallel importation of even genuine goods into Japan and have maintained their monopolistic position regarding the products they handle. On suspicion that this monopoly has prevented a reduction in prices in spite of the revaluation of the yen, the Economic Planning Agency and the Fair Trade Commission have initiated inquiries into the matter.

Against this background, a significant court decision has denied the right of sole agents to enjoin parallel importation of genuine products. This decision was handed down by the Kobe district court on February 27, 1970, and is titled *M.N.C. Inc. v. Shriro Trading Co.* The facts surrounding this case are as follows. The Parker Company, the manufacturer of Parker fountain pens, registered its trademark in Japan and granted an exclusive license to use such mark to the Canadian company which registered the

[58]

right. This company then monopolized the importation of such pens through its distributorship and trademark license. Meanwhile, a Japanese importing company wished to import genuine Parker pens from Hong Kong and was denied permission to do so by the Canadian company. Further, the Canadian company indicated it would not grant permission to any other person when asked by the Custom House about its intentions. The Japanese company brought an action against the Canadian company in the Kobe District Court asking for a declaratory judgement that the defendant has no right to enjoin the importation of genuine goods bearing the registered trademark. The court agreed with the plaintiff, reasoning that the purpose of trademarks is twofold: (1) to guarantee a certain quality of goods and (2) to represent the origin of goods. As long as these two functions are not impeded by an importation, there is no infringement of the domestic trademark. In this case, since the plaintiff was going to import genuine goods bearing genuine trademarks, the importation was not an infringement of the trademark right.

Considering the implications of this decision and the growing opinion against the enforcement of Section 21 of the Tariff Act by the Bureau of Customs, the Ministry of Finance has permitted parallel importation of genuine goods since October 1, 1972. Moreover, it has been reported that domestic prices of some imported products (particularly high-quality liquor) have been lowered considerably lately by the parallel importation of such products by powerful department stores. In the case of some foods, prices have gone down by as much as 40%. Potentially this development could have considerable impact on the method of marketing certain types of goods in Japan.

CONTRACTUAL RESTRICTIONS

A CASE which may prove to be quite significant in international distribution agreements is now pending before the Tokyo High

Court.[13] In this case, Amano Seiyaku Kabushiki Kaisha (Amano), a Japanese company engaged in the production and sale of pharmaceutical products, entered into an international contract with Novo Industri A/S (Novo) for the right to distribute a certain product called ALCALAISE on an exclusive basis in Japan and Okinawa and on a non-exclusive basis in Korea and Taiwan. In the agreement Amano was restricted from: (1) manufacturing and selling competing products for a period of three years after the termination of the contract; (2) selling competing products manufactured by some other company in Japan, Okinawa, Taiwan, or Korea (no term was set for the duration of this obligation); and (3) selling the products at a price less than the minimum resale price established by Novo. Section 6 of the Act provides as follows:

"(1) No entrepreneur shall enter into an international agreement or an international contract which contains such matters as constitute unreasonable restraint of trade or unfair trade practice.

(2) An entrepreneur who has entered into an international agreement or an international contract shall file, in accordance with the regulations of the Fair Trade Commission, a report thereof with the said Commission, accompanied by a copy of the said agreement or contract (in the case of an oral agreement or contract, a document describing the contents thereof), within thirty days as from the execution of such act.

(3) The provisions of the preceding section shall not apply to an agreement or contract regarding a single transaction

---

[13] FTC v. Amano Seiyaku Kabushiki Kaisha, *16 FTC Decision Reports* (1970), p. 134. Additional information concerning this decision can be obtained in M. Kikuchi, *"Dokkinhō Rokujō to Amano Seiyaku Jiken"* ('Section 6 of the Antimonopoly Law and the Amano Seiyaku Case'), in *Kōsei Torihiki 233*, pp. 14–17; S. Tsubota, *"Amano Seiyaku Jiken to Kokusen Kinshihō Rokujō"* ('The Amano Seiyaku Case and Section 6 of the Antimonopoly Act'), *Zaisei Keizai Kōhō*, No. 1345, pp. 9–10; M. Matsushita, "The Antimonopoly Act of Japan and International Transactions", *The Japanese Annual of International Law*, No. 14 (1970), pp. 1 and 13.

(excluding such transactions of which the delivery of the goods extends over a period of one year) or to an agreement or contract merely creating an agency in business matters (excluding an agreement or contract containing conditions that restrict the business activities of the other party)."

Under Section 6 of the Act the contract between Amano and Novo was presented to the Fair Trade Commission for its review and the FTC subsequently issued recommendations to Amano that all three restrictions constituted unreasonable restraints on trade under the *General Designation of Unfair Trade Practices* and requested Amano to eliminate these clauses.[14] Amano responded by cancelling the contract.

Novo, which had not been named in the FTC's recommendations because it had no place of business in Japan and therefore was not subject to the FTC's jurisdiction, instigated an action against the FTC in the Tokyo High Court alleging that it had been denied an opportunity to be heard and therefore the FTC's decision involved an unconstitutional deprivation of due process of law and was null and void. The case is still pending, but the outcome may be significant since it will show the extent of the FTC's power under Section 6 of the Act to invalidate international agreements even though it has jurisdiction only over the injured party and not the injuring party. It also provides insight into the FTC's attitude toward restrictions in agreements between manufacturers and distributors which may constitute unfair business practices.

There are other variations of the basic pattern which may result in a finding of illegality under the Act. For instance, if a powerful trading company were to impose upon small manufacturers the condition that they should not sell their products to others, the

[14] The recommendation advising Amano that the restrictions contained in the contract were considered to be in violation of Section 6 of the Act was issued on December 16, 1969. A recommendation decision ordering Amano to cancel the restrictions was issued on January 12, 1970.

condition might be held illegal under Section 4(8) of the Act. Again, the trading company would have to be quite powerful for this to result. A case which is relevant to these sorts of conditions is *FTC v. Saitama Bank*.[15]

In this case, the Saitama Bank regularly loaned funds to different silk manufacturers who controlled 60% of the silk production in Saitama Prefecture. The general pattern had been for these different silk producers to sell their products to various trading companies. However, the bank began conditioning its loans on a promise from the manufacturers that they would channel all their distributions through a certain trading company which was related to the bank. This, of course, eliminated the previous trading companies. The FTC found that this type of condition imposed on those companies borrowing money from the bank constituted monopolization by the bank and a cease-and-desist order was issued.

Another type of restriction that may be found to be in violation of the Act is territorial restrictions imposed on distributors. As in the other situations which have been mentioned, it is not the simple fact of the agreement which gives rise to the illegality, but rather whether the effect of the agreement is to stifle competition from competitors. If there is a combination of restrictions, such as a territorial restriction or a customer restriction coupled with an exclusive dealing arrangement, the anti-competitive effect would be likely to become significant.

Another example that illustrates the function and the importance of the Act in this general context can be found in some of the practices previously engaged in by department stores. Department stores play a large role in the lives of most urban Japanese and enjoy a tremendous amount of prestige. In Tokyo, masses of people look solely to a few prestige department stores to satisfy the incredible number of gift-giving obligations that constantly arise.

---

[15] FTC v. Saitama Bank, *2 FTC Decision Reports* (1950), p. 74. A similar case involving the production of milk in Hokkaido is FTC v. Yukijirushi (Snow Brand) Milk Products Co., *8 FTC Decision Reports* (1956), p. 12.

The appeal is not the actual quality of the merchandise in a given store so much as the image that the name of the store evokes. Given this role in Japanese society, small manufacturers and wholesalers naturally want to have their commodities exhibited and sold in major department stores, since the very presence of goods in a name department store seems to certify in the minds of many that the goods must be of premium quality. For a while some of the department stores took advantage of this position by demanding that manufacturers or wholesalers desiring to have their goods handled by the store supply personnel to work in the department store at no cost to the store. This practice would seem to run counter to Item 10 of the FTC's *General Designation of Unfair Trade Practices.* However, the FTC chose not to apply the existing law but instead issued a specific notification with regard to department stores which specifically prohibits this practice, at the same time dealing with some additional practices of department stores.[16]

In short, the antimonopoly rules and regulations governing channels of distribution in Japan are not clear-cut but rely heavily on the facts of each particular arrangement. Due to the changes that seem to be taking place in patterns of distribution and in the transfer of power from other government agencies, this may be an area in which the Fair Trade Commission will come to exert a greater degree of influence than it does at present.

Advertisement and sale with premiums

REGULATION of advertising and sales with premiums was originally a matter that was dealt with in Section 2(7) (iii) of the Act on the theory that advertisement and offering unreasonable premiums amount to undue customer inducement. This provision was found to be inadequate when it was discovered that canned meat packaged

---

[16] "Specific Unfair Business Practices in the Department Store Industry," *FTC Notification No. 7* (1954).

in containers showing pictures of cattle and bearing the designation "beef style" was actually whale meat. The FTC countered the problem by enacting a notification covering specific unfair trade practices in the meat-canning industry.[17] However, public indignation rose when it was discovered that this type of misleading advertising was being used in varying degrees throughout a large part of the canned-goods industry in Japan, and the issue was taken up in the Diet. The result was legislation entitled the Act Against Unjustifiable Premiums and Misleading Representation (hereinafter called "Premiums Act").[18] Section 3 of the Premiums Act provides that:

> "The Fair Trade Commission may, when it considers it necessary to prevent unjustifiable inducement of customers, limit the maximum price of a premium or the aggregate amount of premiums, the kind of premium or the method of offering the premium or any other matter relating thereto, or may prohibit the offering of a premium."

Under the authority of this section, the FTC issued Notification 3 of 1962 regulating price contests which defines "premium" to be that which is used as a means of inducing customers and which accompanies the commodity or service that the entrepreneur supplies. This notification specifies four things which constitute premiums. These are

1) goods, land, buildings, and other structures;
2) money, debentures, bonds, and other negotiable instruments;
3) invitations to such things as sports events, movies, trips, etc.;
4) convenience, labor, and other services.

[17] "Specific Unfair Trade Practices in the Animal and Whale Meat, Etc., Canning Industry," *FTC Notification No. 1* (1961).
[18] *Act Against Unjustifiable Premiums and Misleading Representations* (Law No. 134, May 15, 1962).

Chapter Three. Antimonopoly Regulation of Marketing

The FTC also issued Notification 45 of 1962 in which it stipulated maximum amounts for premiums.[19] This sets forth a scale to govern the amounts of premiums offered which varies according to the value of the commodity or service with which the premiums are offered. In some industries, however, premiums are prohibited as a matter of principle.[20] Premiums between traders are regulated elsewhere.[21]

Section 4 of the Premiums Act deals with undue representation including advertisement and labeling of commodities and services. According to this section, a misleading representation is that kind of representation by which quality standards or other matters relating to the substance of the commodity or service may be misunderstood by consumers in general to be much better than the actual ones or than those of competitors dealing in the same commodities and which is likely to induce customers unjustifiably and impede fair competition. (Appendix 5.) An illustrative case which was decided under this law involved a drink known as POKKA LEMON, a lemonade-style soft drink.[22] The advertisements and labels for POKKA LEMON showed pictures of fresh lemons and gave information which suggested that fresh lemons were used in the drink, whereas they were not. The FTC felt that this amounted to undue representation and issued a cease-and-desist order. Under the terms of this

[19] According to this Notification, the maximum amount of a premium is either ¥10,000 or one-twentieth of the price of the commodity or service with which the premium in question is offered, whichever is lower. However, where the value of the commodity or service is below ¥50,000 and above ¥10,000, premiums of ¥30,000 or less can be offered. If the price of the commodity is above ¥100,000, then premiums of ¥50,000 or less can be offered. If the price of the commodity is ¥50, then the maximum premium is an amount derived by multiplying the price, ¥50, by 20, which gives a ¥1,000 maximum premium. If, however, the value of the commodity were ¥600, the multiple by 20 would equal ¥12,000. This would exceed the ¥10,000 limit and therefore the actual premium would be limited to ¥10,000 in this case.

[20] See H. Iyori, *Antimonopoly Legislation in Japan,* New York: Federal Legal Publications, 1969, pp. 82–83.

[21] *FTC Notification No. 17* (1967) sets a limit on the number of premiums a trader may offer in a year.

[22] FTC v. Pokka Lemon, *2 FTC Premiums Decision Reports* (1967), p. 199.

order, the company had to publish a statement in the newspapers that its past advertising and labeling policies were illegal and that it had been ordered by the FTC to discontinue such representations. The POKKA LEMON bottle now exhibits a statement that artificial flavoring is used in the drink.

Besides specifying regulations concerning premiums and representations, another function of the Premiums Act was to simplify legal procedures. If the FTC desires, it can avoid regular proceedings and hold a simple hearing. The accused party has the opportunity to defend himself at the hearing, but the procedures for the hearing are designed to be simple and quick. As a result of the hearing, a cease-and-desist order may be issued. (Premiums Act, Section 5–9.)

The existence of Fair Competition Codes should be mentioned as another exception to the Antimonopoly Act which potentially could grow in significance. This is a means whereby entrepreneurs in a certain industry can agree upon how competition should be carried out in that industry and can establish their own fair competition code. This code should be submitted to the FTC for its approval. Once FTC approval has been obtained, the rules of the Code are exempt from the application of the Antimonopoly Act and can be enforced through legal processes. This is a type of self-regulation of competition which can be very effective at times.

The Premiums Act has played an important role in the protection of consumers from misleading and deceptive marketing techniques. With the current development in awareness of the rights of consumers in Japan, it seems reasonable to anticipate further activity in administrative and judicial interpretation of this law and promulgation of official notifications to supplement it.

CONCLUSION

THIS discussion has been limited solely to marketing in Japan and has not dealt with several other areas where the role of Japanese antimonopoly law has been significant. Even within this limited approach, the degree of power the antimonopoly law and its chief guardian, the FTC, wields in the world of Japanese business is striking, especially in view of the fact that the basic law was artificially grafted on to a social structure which had never embraced many of the ideals that served as the underlying base for the growth of this type of legislation in the West.

The place of the FTC and the role of antimonopoly legislation have had periods of highs and lows during their brief history in Japan. While it seems at last to be firmly established as a Japanese institution, the FTC is still a center of controversy in both Japanese and foreign business circles. The present outlook, however, is for the FTC to play a key role in the life of all businesses marketing in Japan during the 1970s. This role may be strengthened by the prognosis for change in traditional Japanese marketing patterns and a gradual relaxation of control over the activities of foreign business by other Japanese government agencies. Also, the ambiguities surrounding the jurisdiction of the Antimonopoly Act seem likely to be resolved in favor of extending the reach of the Act as illustrated by the FTC's actions in the *Amano* case.

One blessing of the Antimonopoly Act is that it is a two-edged sword that exacts the same degree of care from Japanese and foreign business alike. Hopefully it will continue to contribute to the development of a climate where Japanese and foreign business can work and compete in harmony with each other.

Appendices

APPENDIX I
Act Concerning Prohibition of Private Monopoly and Maintenance of Fair Trade (Act No. 54, April 14, 1947).
Section 2(7) reads as follows:
 The term "unfair business practices" as used in this act shall mean any act coming

under any one of the following paragraphs which tends to impede fair competition and which is designated by the Fair Trade Commission.

   i) Unduly discriminating against other entrepreneurs;

   ii) Dealing at undue prices;

   iii) Unreasonably inducing or coercing customers of a competitor to deal with oneself;

   iv) Trading with another party on such conditions as will restrict unjustly the business activities of the said party;

   v) Dealing with another party by unwarranted use of one's bargaining position;

   vi) Unjustly interfering with a transaction between an entrepreneur who competes in Japan with oneself or the company of which oneself is a stockholder or an officer and his customers; or, in case such entrepreneur is a company, unjustly inducing, instigating, or coercing a stockholder or an officer of such company to act against the interest of such company.

APPENDIX 2

Fair Trade Commission Notification No. 11 (1953).

In accordance with the provisions of Section 2(7) of the *Act Concerning Prohibition of Private Monopoly and Maintenance of Fair Trade* (Act No. 54 of 1947), unfair business practices, other than specific business practices in a particular field of trade to be designated in accordance with the procedure as provided for in Section 71 of said Act, shall be designated as follows:

UNFAIR BUSINESS PRACTICES

   1) Unduly refusing or limiting deliveries from certain entrepreneurs or to supply to certain other entrepreneurs, commodities, funds, or other kinds of economic benefit.

   2) Affording, without good reason, substantially favorable or unfavorable treatment to certain entrepreneurs in regard to the terms or execution of transactions.

   3) Excluding certain entrepreneurs from concerted activities or from a trade association, or unduly discriminating against specific entrepreneurs in the concerted activities of the trade association, thereby causing to such entrepreneurs undue disadvantage with respect to their business activities.

   4) Supplying or receiving without good cause, commodities, funds, or other kinds of economic benefit at prices which discriminate between customers in different places or between customers.

   5) Supplying commodities, funds, or other kinds of economic benefit at unreasonably low prices or receiving them at unreasonably high prices.

   6) Inducing or coercing, directly or indirectly, customers of a competitor to deal with oneself by offering undue advantages or threatening undue disadvantages in the light of normal business practices.

   7) Dealing with customers on the condition that they shall, without good cause, not supply commodities, funds, or other kinds of economic benefit from a competitor of oneself.

8) Dealing with customers on conditions which, without good reason, restrict any transaction between the said customers and the supplier of commodities, funds, or other kinds of economic benefit to them or between the said customers and any person receiving those from them, or any relationship between the said customer and their competitors.

9) Dealing with a company on the condition, without good reason, that the appointment of officers of that company, meaning those as defined by subsection (3) of Section 2 of the *Act Concerning the Prohibition of Private Monopoly and Maintenance of Fair Trade*, shall be subject to prior direction or approval by oneself.

10) Trading with customers on conditions which are unduly unfavorable in the light of normal business practices by making use of one's predominant position over the said customers.

11) Unjustly interfering with a transaction between other entrepreneurs who compete in Japan with oneself or with the company of which oneself is a stockholder or an officer and their party to such transaction by preventing the execution of a contract, or by inducing breach of contract, or by any other means whatsoever.

12) Unjustly inducing, abetting, or coercing a stockholder or an officer of a company which competes in Japan with oneself or a company of which oneself is a stockholder or an officer, to act against the interest of such company by the exercise of voting rights, transfer of stock, divulgence of secrets, or any other means whatsoever.

APPENDIX 3

Customs Tariff Law (Law No. 54, 1010) Art. 9 reads as follows:

If, in case a complaint has been filed that the import of dumped goods or the dumping of imported goods would or might cause damage to a Japanese industry or will arrest the firm establishment of a Japanese industry, the government has affirmed the fact of dumping and deems it necessary for the protection of the industry concerned, customs duty equivalent to the difference between the fair price and the dumping price of the goods concerned may be imposed in addition to the customs duty at the rate as prescribed in the separate table (as regards ad valorem dutiable goods and ad valorem and specific dutiable goods, customs duty in an amount computed with the fair price taken as the dutiable value) with goods and the period of time designated, in accordance with the provisions of the Cabinet Order. (Omitted.)

APPENDIX 4

General Agreement on Tariffs and Trade (GATT), TIAS 1700 (1947).
Article VI. Anti-dumping and Countervailing Duties.

1) The contracting parties recognize that dumping, by which products of one country are introduced into the commerce of another country at less than the normal value of the products, is to be condemned if it causes or threatens material injury to an established industry in the territory of a contracting party or materially retards the establishment

of a domestic industry. For the purposes of this Article, a product is to be considered as being introduced into the commerce of an importing country at less than its normal value if the price of the product exported from one country to another (a) is less than the comparable price, in the ordinary course of trade, for the like product when destined for consumption in the exporting country, or, (b) in the absence of such domestic price, is less than either

i) the highest comparable price for the like product for export to any third country in the ordinary course of trade, or

ii) the cost of production of the product in the country of origin plus a reasonable addition for selling cost and profit. Due allowance shall be made in each case for differences in conditions and terms of sale, for differences in taxation, and for other differences affecting price comparability.

2) In order to offset or prevent dumping, a contracting party may levy on any dumped product an anti-dumping duty not greater in amount than the margin of dumping in respect of such product. For the purposes of this Article, the margin of dumping is the price difference determined in accordance with the provisions of Paragraph 1.

3) (Omitted.)

4) No product of the territory of any contracting party imported into the territory of any other contracting party shall be subject to anti-dumping or countervailing duty by reason of the exemption of such product from duties or taxes borne by the like product when destined for consumption in the country of origin or exportation, or by reason of the refund of such duties or taxes.

5) No product of the territory of a contracting party imported into the territory of any other contracting party shall be subject to both anti-dumping and countervailing duties to compensate for the same situation of dumping or export subsidization.

6) No contracting party shall levy anti-dumping or countervailing duty on the importation of any product of the territory of another contracting party unless it determines that the effect of the dumping or subsidization, as the case may be, is such as to cause or threaten material injury to an established domestic industry, or is such as to retard materially the establishment of a domestic industry . . .

APPENDIX 5

Act Against Unjustifiable Premiums and Misleading Representations
Section 4 reads as follows:

No entrepreneur shall make such representations as provided for in the following paragraph in connection with transactions regarding a commodity or service which he supplies:

i) Any representation by which the quality, standard or any other matter relating to the substance of a commodity or service will be misunderstood by consumers in general to be much better than the actual one or than that of other entrepreneurs who are in competition with the entrepreneur, and which is likely to induce customers unjustifiably and to impede fair competition;

ii) Any representation by which price or any other term of sale of a commodity or service will be misunderstood by consumers in general to be substantially more favorable to customers than the actual one or than that of other entrepreneurs who are in competition with the entrepreneur, and which is likely to induce customers unjustifiably and to impede fair competition;

iii) In addition to those mentioned in the preceding two paragraphs, any representation by which any matter relating to transactions as to a commodity or service is likely to be misunderstood by consumers in general and which is designated by the Fair Trade Commission as tending to induce customers unjustifiably and to impede fair competition.

Part II

THE JAPANESE CONSUMER

CHAPTER FOUR

How Homogeneous is the Japanese Market?

HIDEO GOTŌ

Geographical structure and population—Size and standards of markets—Trends in consumer markets—Markets by income and age levels

THE high-powered economic growth of Japan after the Second World War was supported by the industrial development of the three regions of Kanto (the area including the largest metropolitan area, Tokyo), Kinki (the area including the second largest metropolitan area, Osaka-Kobe), and Tokai (the area including Nagoya). Seventy-five per cent of the national industrial output and 60% of the Japanese population are concentrated in these areas, which are showing signs of over-saturation. The outlying areas, in the meantime, are becoming urbanized in giant strides. Together with the remarkable economic growth of these three areas, the rural districts are also getting rapidly industrialized. This phenomenon is especially apparent in the so-called "Pacific Belt Zone" which comprises the broad strip of coastal land extending from Tokyo to northern Kyushu and includes the three large industrial centers mentioned above. However, while the rural industrial output is increasing year by year in absolute quantity, its share of national production is trending downward. Also, when the Keihin (Tokyo-Yokohama) and Hanshin (Osaka-Kobe) industrial areas are compared, it is clear that Keihin's share is increasing yearly, whereas Hanshin's share has remained somewhat static.

Agriculture is the most important industry in the less industrialized areas. However, since young labor now tends to be absorbed by the secondary and tertiary industries in the large cities, the growth rate of agricultural production is small. The decrease in agricultural population in the Pacific Belt Zone is due to the fact that full-time farming households are shifting to part-time farming, and in the areas other than the Pacific Belt Zone there is a general exodus of people towards large cities.

On the other hand, the rapid development of transportation and communications systems has brought the rural areas and large cities into ever closer contact and emphasized the latter's role as centers of commerce and administration. This importance is made clear from the single fact that these three areas occupy 80% of the national wholesale trade.

The position of Tokyo, which used to be somewhat inferior to Osaka in economic terms (though always the leader in terms of government and administration), has recently come to surpass Osaka and has assumed the leading position in terms of commerce and production as well as administration. And this development has in turn spurred on its growth into a gigantic metropolis.

Geographical structure and population

IF the industrial structure of the Japanese economy is divided into nine geographical regions (Exhibit 1), each can be reviewed from the point of view of the ratio of people engaged in primary, secondary, and tertiary industries. (Exhibit 2.) The three industrial regions, Kanto, Kinki, and Tokai, have a similar industrial structure with a large proportion of the population engaged in secondary

Chapter Four. How Homogeneous is the Japanese Market?

EXHIBIT I

JAPAN'S REGIONS, PREFECTURES, MAIN CITIES AND TRADITIONAL SUB-REGIONS

REGIONS	PREFECTURES	MAIN CITIES	TRADITIONAL SUB-REGIONS
CHUGOKU	Hiroshima	Hiroshima, Kure	
	Okayama	Okayama	
	Shimane	Matsue	
	Tottori	Tottori	
	Yamaguchi	Yamaguchi, Shimonoseki	
HOKKAIDO	Hokkaido	Sapporo, Hakodate	
HOKURIKU	Fukui	Fukui	
	Ishikawa	Kanazawa	
	Niigata	Niigata, Tsubame	
	Toyama	Toyama	
KANTO	Chiba	Chiba, Tateyama	Keihin
	Gumma	Maebashi	(Tokyo, Yokohama)
	Ibaraki	Mito, Hitachi	
	Kanagawa	Yokohama, Kawasaki	
	Saitama	Urawa	
	Tochigi	Utsunomiya	
	Tokyo	Tokyo	
KINKI	Hyogo	Kobe	Keihanshin
	Kyoto	Kyoto	(Kyoto, Osaka,
	Nara	Nara	Kobe)
	Osaka	Osaka	
	Shiga	Otsu	Hanshin
	Wakayama	Wakayama	(Osaka, Kobe)
KYUSHU	Fukuoka	Fukuoka, Kita-Kyushu	
	Kagoshima	Kagoshima	
	Kumamoto	Kumamoto	
	Miyazaki	Miyazaki, Nobeoka	
	Nagasaki	Nagasaki, Sasebo	
	Oita	Oita, Beppu	
	Saga	Saga	

[77]

SHIKOKU	Ehime	Matsuyama	
	Kagawa	Takamatsu	
	Kochi	Kochi	
	Tokushima	Tokushima	
TOHOKU	Akita	Akita	
	Aomori	Aomori, Hirosaki	
	Fukushima	Fukushima, Wakamatsu	
	Iwate	Morioka	
	Miyagi	Sendai	
	Yamagata	Yamagata	
TOKAI	Aichi	Nagoya	Chukyo
	Gifu	Gifu, Takayama	(Aichi, Gifu,
	Mie	Tsu	Mie)
	Nagano	Nagano, Matsumoto	
	Shizuoka	Shizuoka, Hamamatsu	
	Yamanashi	Kofu	
RYUKYU	Okinawa	Naha	

and tertiary industries. Among the three, the Tokai region has a relatively larger population engaged in primary industry.

Of the other six regions, Hokkaido has the smallest share of primary industries and, despite its importance as an agricultural producer, a large proportion of tertiary industries. That its tertiary population ratio is even larger than that of the Kinki region probably indicates its relative economic independence, which is due to the geographic fact that it is farthest away from mainland industrial centers. The Chugoku, Hokuriku, and Shikoku regions all have about the same industrial population ratio. In Chugoku, which is part of the Pacific Belt Zone, there is a larger portion of people engaged in secondary industries. Kyushu, which covers the south-end of the Pacific Belt Zone and the southern agricultural districts, has a larger proportion in primary and tertiary industries. In the Tohoku region the proportion of population in secondary and tertiary industries is small as compared with that in primary industries; this is the main agricultural district of Japan.

[78]

EXHIBIT 2
POPULATION 15 AND OVER IN PRIMARY,
SECONDARY, AND TERTIARY INDUSTRIES, BY REGION
(1970)

REGIONS	TOTAL		PRIMARY	SECONDARY	TERTIARY
	Thousand	%			
ALL JAPAN	52,425	100	19.3%	33.9%	46.7%
CHUGOKU	3,735	100	27.0	29.6	43.4
HOKKAIDO	2,439	100	21.4	24.6	54.0
HOKURIKU	2,799	100	25.8	33.5	40.8
KANTO	14,695	100	19.3	36.4	44.3
KINKI	8,485	100	15.0	37.8	47.2
KYUSHU	5,662	100	32.4	21.7	45.9
SHIKOKU	2,030	100	30.0	25.8	44.3
TOHOKU	4,539	100	39.3	21.3	39.3
TOKAI	7,659	100	22.0	36.8	41.2
OKINAWA	382	100	23.6	19.1	57.3

Source: *Minryoku 1972* ('National Resources 1972'), Tokyo: Asahi Shimbun-sha, 1972, p. 50.

Because of the relative economic positions of these different areas, the population has been shifting from the districts of low productivity (primary) industries to those of higher productivity (secondary and tertiary) industries and is now concentrated in the latter areas. In 1971, of the 105.4 million population of Japan about 40% were gathered in and around the three large industrial centers. There were 16.7 million (16%) in the Keihin area, 14.5 million (13.9%) in the Keihanshin area, and 8.8 million (8.4%) in the Chukyo area. The more broadly defined Pacific Belt Zone contained 70.1 million persons, or 67.1% of the entire Japanese population. Furthermore, while the average (median) population density in Japan was 282.5 persons per sq km, that in Tokyo was 5,225.4 per sq km and in Osaka 4,070.6 persons per sq km.[1]

Although, during the five years between 1965–1970, the Japanese population increased by 5.4 million (a growth rate of 5.4%), there

[1] *Minryoku 1972* ('National Resources'), Tokyo: Asahi Shimbun-sha, 1972, p. 41.

were considerable differences between the growth rates of various areas. Population expansion was most remarkable in the Keihin area with a growth of 1.6 million during the five years; Keihanshin expanded by 1.5 million, and Chukyo by 0.7 million. The population growth of these districts is mainly due to the urbanization of the suburban areas either for industrial or bed-town purposes. To take one example, while the population of Tokyo Prefecture itself grew by only 5% during the five years, that of the surrounding three prefectures grew by as much as 25%. Outside the three central areas, population growth has also occurred in middle-sized cities such as Sapporo, Sendai, Hiroshima, and Fukuoka. As the economic center of Hokkaido, Sapporo especially has grown remarkably.

On the other hand, within the vast areas outside of these industrial centers, the population is becoming sparser year by year. As already noted, people are moving out of the rural areas into the large cities in several discernible flows—those in eastern Japan flock to the Keihin area and those in western Japan to the Hanshin area. Chukyo, which is situated in between those two great industrial zones, absorbs what is left of the shifting mass of migrating population. While Hokkaido is included in eastern Japan, it suffers from a smaller population decrease than other areas.

The shift in population is mainly due to the employment of young people newly graduated from schools. And this means that the median age in the rural districts is becoming higher, while that in large cities is coming down. For instance, 19% of the total population of Japan is aged between 20–29, whereas that age range is 25% in the Keihin area and 22% in Keihanshin and Chukyo areas. In contrast, only 15% of the Tohoku region, which suffers from a great loss of population, are aged 20–29. The young workers who settle in large cities eventually become, together with their growing families, an important factor in enlarging the consumer market of the metropolitan areas.

Chapter Four. How Homogeneous is the Japanese Market?

Size and standards of markets

THE size of the Japanese consumer market expressed in terms of individual consumption expenditures was $87,000 million ($1.00 =¥360) in total in 1969. Of this amount, Keihin and the surrounding areas accounted for 29%, Keihanshin 17%, and Chukyo 8%, for a total of 54%. If we include the entire Pacific Belt Zone, the share of individual consumption expenditures becomes 69%. This concentration of consumption into specific areas is thus greater than that of population.

In terms of the retail sales breakdown, in 1970, 20.8% was accounted for by Keihin, 15.5% by Keihanshin, and 8.7% by Chukyo. These three areas combined accounted for about 45% of national sales, and the retail sales of the Pacific Belt Zone accounted for 72%.[2]

A considerable difference exists in the size of consumer markets of the nine geographical regions: Kanto 28%, Kinki 17%, Tokai 14%, and Kyushu 10%; the shares of Tohoku, Hokuriku, Hokkaido, and Chugoku are small: 9%, 5%, 5%, and 7% respectively.

The consumer market analyzed in terms of the kind of merchandise sold becomes as follows. With respect to "clothes and apparel" Keihin occupies 20%, Keihanshin 15%, and Chukyo 8%, totalling 43%. These three areas also occupy 44% of the "food and beverages" market, with 57% of meat and egg sales and 60% of milk sales. The shares of these three areas in the "furniture and electrical household appliances" market are 44%. The fact that the latter shares are as great as those in clothing or food and beverage markets is probably due to the fact that when the demand for electrical household appliances reaches a saturation point in the large cities it shifts to the rural districts. Other items which have greater markets in these three areas are cosmetics (49%),

2 *Ibid.*, p. 68.

pharmaceutical goods (53%), automobiles (41%), cameras and watches (47%). The reason why western-style food, cosmetics, and passenger cars are in greater demand in the large cities as compared with the rural areas is that young people with high living standards are concentrated in the cities. The fact that the percentages of individual consumption expenditures and the amount of retail business carried on in large cities exceeds the ratio of their population concentration testifies to the high level of urban income and expenditure.

It is possible to study these geographical differences by the household expenditures in each region. The national average for household expenditures per month was ¥79,531 in 1970. Local differences spread from ¥86,531 (Kanto) to ¥67,260 (Kyushu). (Exhibit 3.)

EXHIBIT 3
AVERAGE MONTHLY HOUSEHOLD EXPENDITURES BY REGION
(1970)

REGIONS	MONTHLY HOUSEHOLD EXPENDITURES
ALL JAPAN	¥79,531
KANTO	86,531
(Keihin)	(89,154)
KINKI	81,537
(Keihanshin)	(82,688)
HOKKAIDO	75,752
TOKAI	78,948
(Chukyo)	(81,250)
CHUGOKU	78,023
HOKURIKU	77,368
TOHOKU	73,330
SHIKOKU	67,550
KYUSHU	¥67,260

Source: *Kakei Chōsa Nenpō 1970* ('Annual Report on the Family Income and Expenditure Survey'), Tokyo: Bureau of Statistics, 1971, p. 64.

Chapter Four. How Homogeneous is the Japanese Market?

Trends in consumer markets

THE household expenditures at the national level are given in Exhibit 4. In order, however, to get a clearer picture of the differences that exist between each region, one should examine more minutely the ratio occupied by various items of household expenditures.

EXHIBIT 4
PERCENTAGE OF HOUSEHOLD EXPENDITURES BY MAIN ITEMS
(1970)

ITEMS	ALL HOUSEHOLDS	ALL WORKERS' HOUSEHOLDS
Food	34.1%	32.2%
Housing	10.6	11.2
Fuel and light	3.9	3.7
Clothing	10.8	10.7
Miscellaneous	40.6	42.2

Source: *Kakei Chōsa Nenpō 1970* ('Annual Report on Family Income and Expenditure Survey'), Tokyo: Bureau of Statistics, 1971, pp. 82–91.

With respect to food, rice accounts for the greatest share of expenditure in every region. In Kanto, however, the percentage of rice purchased is somewhat smaller than in the other regions. The amount of bread consumed is considerably less than that of rice (1/7 of rice on national average). In Kanto and Kinki, the proportion of expenditure on bread is a little larger (1/6 of rice) than the national average. It may be concluded that Japanese dietary habits still emphasize rice as the main staple food.

In respect to fish or meat and eggs, more of the latter category are purchased in Kanto, Tokai, Kinki, Chugoku, and Kyushu. In reverse, more money is expended on fish than on meat or eggs in Hokuriku, Tohoku, Hokkaido, and Shikoku. The amount of sales of meat is especially high in the Kinki region, and the share of vegetables is also high in Kanto and Kinki (due to the fact that vegetables are more expensive in large cities than in rural districts).

[83]

Processed foods (bean-curd, canned goods, fried foods, fish sausages, etc.) are sold more in the Tokai and Kinki regions, while cakes and candies, tea, coffee, cider, juice, and alcoholic beverages have a greater market in eastern Japan. For the rest, more people eat out in Kanto.

As between Kanto and Kinki, the latter households spend a greater share of their living expenses on rice, fish, meat, and eggs. At least a part of the old saying, "Osaka goes bankrupt spending too much on food; Kyoto goes bankrupt over clothes," is manifested here.

Other than foodstuffs, the share occupied by rental fees for house and/or land is especially large in the Kanto region, including the Keihin area. The over-concentration of population in and around this area has resulted in an acute housing shortage, which in turn is proving a great burden to family expenditures. The ratio of expenditures on furniture and electrical household appliances is higher in the regions with lower expenditure levels. This shows that the high percentage of household ownership, for instance, of television sets (75.1 B/W and 61.1 color sets in February 1972) in Japan is not necessarily indicative of high living standards.[3]

Of the light and fuel fees, city gas is not generally used in regions other than Kanto and Kinki, and the former mostly rely on coal, charcoal, kerosene, or propane gas.

No great difference is observed with respect to clothing and apparel among the regions. No matter which Japanese city is cited, people wear about the same kind of clothes. The development of mass communications seems to have eradicated local color.

However, the share of culture and entertainment is high in Kanto and Kinki, reflecting the brilliance of city life. Furthermore, the greatness of the share of transportation fees in the Kanto region indicates the distance between people's place of work and their

[3] *Shōhi-sha Dōkō Yosoku Chōsa Sokuhō, Feb. 1972* ('Preliminary Report of Consumers' Intentions on Household Spending, Feb. 1972'), Tokyo: Economic Planning Agency, 1972, p. 7.

homes. The fact that the share of educational fees is large in Kanto while that of remittance is great in Tohoku, Hokuriku, Chugoku, and Shikoku, etc. means that a great number of young people are sent to Tokyo for their education.

The fact that 99.3% of the national population is Japanese, with only 718,795 persons out of 105.4 million being of foreign extraction,[4] helps to keep the homogeneous characteristics of the Japanese nation comparatively intact. With respect to language, even though local dialects still do exist, the development of mass communications has spread the use of standard Japanese to the extent that most people speak it, and some old dialects are disappearing. On the other hand, however, some dialects such as those used in Osaka or Kyoto have been made more familiar to the rest of Japan through mass communications. In any event, we may say that no language barrier exists between various parts of Japan.

With respect to the way in which a "family" is considered, a noticeable amount of difference is observed between those educated before World War II and after it. According to the Family Law enacted in 1947, more emphasis has come to be placed on the relationship between husband and wife than on parents and children. In 1970 the size of family on the national average was 3.98 persons; for Tohoku 4.00, Hokuriku 4.02, Keihin and Chukyo 4.05, and Keihanshin 3.96.[5] Furthermore, the fact that large cities have a greater number of young people and that conversely rural districts have more people of advanced age would naturally result in different attitudes towards "family" between these areas, which should in turn reflect themselves in their consumption patterns. Acceptance of western goods or attitudes towards culture and entertainment may very well conflict with the traditional ideas held by the older people residing in rural areas.

---

4 In 1971, out of a total of 718,795 foreigners, 622,690 were Korean and 52,333 Chinese. (*Jinkō Suikei Geppō,* Feb. 1972 ['Monthly Report On Current Population Estimates, Feb. 1972']), Tokyo: Bureau of Statistics, 1972, p. 6.
5 *Kakei Chōsa Nenpō 1970, op. cit.,* p. 106.

With the disintegration of the patriarchal system in the cities, the economic powers within the household were transferred into the hands of women. The emphasis placed on the "women's hour" by the mass communications media, wives participating in ladies' programs, the energy displayed by women at the bargain counters of department stores, housewives with more leisure owing to the spread of electrical household appliances, and the appearance of husbands on a "hundred yen a day allowance" all testify to the growing consumer market centering around housewives.

People, however, maintain conservative habits in certain aspects of life. As related before, rice remains the main staple food for the Japanese, and national costume still holds sway among elderly ladies. Especially in large housing areas, people generally use tables and chairs in their dining-kitchens, but in sleeping, relaxing, and entertaining guests, most still resort to the traditional use of *tatami*. In considering the promotion of the Japanese consumer market, one must always bear in mind these leanings towards traditional ways, which are inherent both in urban and rural areas.

A great difference can be observed in the purchasing patterns between people of Tokyo and Osaka. For instance, there are many large monthly installment stores in Tokyo which advertise "Play now, pay later." But there are very few of them in Osaka. Osakans always pay cash for their durable consumer goods; rather than buy a ¥50,000 TV set through installment payments of 10 months, they would wait out the period and buy the set at a discount. The stores in Tokyo pay more attention to decorating their show windows attractively than to displaying the merchandise itself. The stores in Osaka load their show-cases with goods and try to attract customers by the rich variety of their merchandise. The restaurants in Osaka list the prices of their menu at the front, while in Tokyo people have the idea that the more high class the restaurant the more concealed are its prices. We can conclude that Tokyo residents are vain and spendthrift, while Osaka residents are down-to-earth and practical.

Chapter Four. How Homogeneous is the Japanese Market?

Nevertheless, with progress in transportation the geographical differences among Japanese will eventually disappear, as the increasing flow of people from the rural districts to large cities will erase any regional characteristics they have. The pattern of consumption will become increasingly uniform in the future.

Markets by income and age levels

THERE are 24.6 million households with more than two members and 6.9 million single-member households in Japan (1971). (Exhibit 5.) How much purchasing power do these households have? If a margin is set at households with incomes of about $2,270 ($1.00= ¥270) a year, 13% of the total households in Japan cannot be considered potential consumers. Households, on the other hand, with yearly incomes of over $9,300 (¥2.5 million) amount only to 11%. This means that the bulk of the Japanese consumer market is composed of families which must of necessity budget their incomes. Although most households own one or more TV sets, it does not follow that they are ready and able to buy almost everything else.

EXHIBIT 5
NUMBER OF HOUSEHOLDS BY SIZE
AND YEARLY INCOME BRACKET
(1971)

SIZE	YEARLY INCOME BRACKET	NUMBER OF HOUSEHOLDS
Single member		6,686,000
Two or more members		24,636,000
Of the latter	less than ¥290,000	1,179,000
	300,000 to 590,000	1,964,000
	600,000 to 990,000	5,582,000
	1,000,000 to 1,490,000	6,971,000
	1,500,000 to 2,490,000	6,216,000
	¥2,500,000 or more	2,689,000

Source: *Shūgyō Kōzō Kihon Chōsa Hōkoku, 1971* ('Employment Status Survey'), Tokyo: Bureau of Statistics, 1972, p. 326.

If urban residents are divided into 5 groups of equal size according to their income level, they show the following household expenditures in 1970:

Group i. Lowest income group, with an annual household expenditure of ¥576,408 (average number of family 3.41 members); 40.4% of their expenditures is spent on food. They are barely making a living.

Group ii. Next lowest income group, with an annual household expenditure of ¥777,288 (3.78 persons). Their food expenditure is 37.1%, which is still large. Their household budgets have to be centered around food.

Group iii. Middle group, with average household expenditure of ¥916,032 (4.00 persons). Their food expenditure is 34.8%.

Group iv. Second from the top group, with annual household expenditure of ¥1,057,608 (4.20 persons). Their food expenses are 33.4%. They have some latitude in spending money on things other than food.

Group v. Highest group, with household expenditure amounting to ¥1,358,184 (4.50 persons). Their food expenses are as low as 30.2%. They spend proportionately more on education, culture, and entertainment.[6]

In Japan, twice-yearly bonuses (usually in June and December) are given in addition to regular salaries. The amount of bonuses is generally 2–5 times the monthly wages, and this practice makes it possible two times a year for people to purchase electrical household appliances, expensive clothes, cameras, or engage in the so-called "leisure activities". When the middle-income bracket people have acquired all the electrical appliances they require, they probably will begin to purchase passenger cars. In the case of such large items, they make down-payments and pay the rest in monthly installments. However, Japanese expenditures on many consumer items

[6] *Ibid.*, p. 107.

are still far below the international standard, e.g. daily food. Per capita consumption of calories and protein in Japan is small because daily food cannot be bought all at one time with the bonus. Another item that the bonus cannot cover is a "house". A great many people share one room and most of the houses do not have flush toilets. People in the middle-income bracket, which includes the bulk of Japanese households, economize on food, resign themselves to crowded living quarters, but dress fashionably, watch TV, use vacuum cleaners, and move around in their own cars. While this unique consumption pattern is not entirely caused by bonus alone, still its role in the Japanese market cannot be minimized.

When the Japanese population is divided into the age groups of 0–14, 15–59, and 60 and over, it appears that the 0–14 group is diminishing year by year, while the 60 and over group is increasing. They number, respectively, 25 million, 68 million, and 11 million at present, but are expected to become 22 million, 72 million, and 24 million by 1990. The growth of an aged population may give birth to a new market in the future, but currently old people are mostly dependent on the younger generation economically and so cannot be counted as a likely market.

The general market composed of people aged 15–59 can be divided into family markets centering on households and youth markets made up of single men and women and students. As the average age of marriage for men is 27 and for women 24, the number of people in the age bracket between middle school graduation and marriage becomes roughly 20 million. This age group includes the mass that was born during the postwar baby-boom period of 1947–1950. Within a few years they will get married and form a new family market, and the size of the youth market will probably settle at about 16 million or so.

Because of the recent economic expansion and the resultant labor shortage, the starting salary of Japanese workers has been rising from year to year, and for this reason we may consider the youth market to be extremely hopeful. (Exhibit 6.) The young people who have experienced a high standard of living tend to carry it over into their married lives, which the older generation cannot understand, because the outcome often results in a so-called "one-point luxury system" (i.e. skimp on food and buy a passenger car, stereophonic equipment, or a piano).

EXHIBIT 6

AVERAGE YEARLY INCOME BY YOUNGER
AGE BRACKET (MALE)
(1971)

AGE BRACKET	NATIONAL AVERAGE	NON–AGRICULTURAL AVERAGE
15–19	¥ 460,000	¥ 460,000
20–24	639,000	639,000
25–29	855,000	856,000
30–34	1,036,000	1,038,000
35–39	1,147,000	1,152,000

Source: *Shūgyō Kōzō Kihon Chōsa Hōkoku, 1971* ('Employment Status Survey'), Tokyo: Bureau of Statistics, 1972, p. 138.

The average annual income of young working girls is ¥477,000. Though the amount is small, since most of them live with and/or are dependent on their parents, most of their income is expended as pocket money, i.e. for clothes, cosmetics, jewelry, amusement, eating out, trips, or savings for trousseau, and the like.

Married employed workers number 34.5 million, of whom 23.4 million are men and 11.1 million are women.[7] Many of the women work to help their family trade, either in agriculture or commerce. And when they get married, they acquire the purse-strings of the household and become the mainstay of the family market. However, because nearly 20% of the urban working couples live with their parents, newlyweds do not immediately constitute a new market. But since roughly one million weddings take place a year (1,029,405 in 1970), the value of the bridal market is considerable. Next most

[7] *Shūgyō Kōzō Kihon Chōsa Hōkoku, 1971, op. cit.,* p. 42.

important is the baby market, with about 1.9 million births a year (1,932,849 in 1970).[8] The value of the second or later child as a potential market is not as great as that of the firstborn, since it is a custom nowadays to spend lavishly on the firstborn.

After the initial expenditure on newborn babies, Japanese parents may enjoy a brief period of economic relaxation. Still, once the children reach school age, the expenses on their food and education begin to mount, and the parents can hardly be expected to spend money on anything else. The number of primary and middle school pupils, though on a diminishing trend, still amounts to 14 million (14,289,427 in May 1971)[9] and, with their educational fees and pocket money, etc., constitutes a sizable market. Furthermore, since children are easily influenced by television, they also can become a determining factor in family spending.

High school and college students numbering 6 million constitute a unique market with their educational fees, pocket money, and part-time work income. However, their living standards are largely influenced by those of their parents and too much cannot be expected of them. They will eventually go to work. But the young men of this country do not have much illusion about their future work or social success, and consequently do not go out of their way to struggle with reality. Instead, they satisfy their wants by acquiring minor items within their reach. This constitutes the youth market, the members of which gradually advance towards the bridal market, thus continuing the infinite life cycle.

---

[8] *Jinkō Dōtai Tōkei Geppō, 1970 Nen-kei* ('Population Vital Statistics, Cumulative 1970'), Tokyo: Ministry of Health & Welfare, 1971, p. 8.

[9] *Minryoku 1972, op. cit.,* p. 126.

CHAPTER FIVE

Seaweed or Bread for Breakfast?

ANDREW WATT AND MIHOKO AIHARA

Overall trends—Kitchen facilities and cooking methods—What's on the menu? bread; fish; meat; vegetables and fruit; dairy products; soup products; soft drinks; tea and coffee; confectionery and snack foods—Receptivity to innovation

IN Colombia about 70% of the average household's budget goes for food. In the U.S. it is around 25%. This ratio, the Engel's coefficient (expenditure on food as a percentage of total expenditure), has long been taken as a rough guide to a country's stage in development, with households in the richer countries being able to satisfy their food needs with a smaller proportion of their available funds. Japan's Engel's coefficient has been decreasing for a number of years. For non-farm households it has dropped from 53.4% in 1953 to 33.4% in 1971.[1] (This does not of course mean an absolute drop in food expenditure, since the average household's expenditure has gone up in real terms over the same period.)

As the proportion of the family budget spent on food has decreased, the standard of nutrition has improved. And the Japanese have shown considerable flexibility and receptivity to innovation

---

[1] *Kakei Chōsa Hōkoku*, Dec. 1971 ('Monthly Report on the Family Income and Expenditure Survey'), Tokyo: Bureau of Statistics, 1972, p. 69.

as new types of food have become standard items on the menu of millions of Japanese households.

In this chapter, a broad picture is given of Japanese food consumption trends and cooking methods; a number of specific product fields are then considered, emphasis being placed on fields where the consumption pattern has significantly changed or developed in the past ten or fifteen years.

Overall trends

THE history of the Japanese diet after the war may be divided into three main phases.

a) First, the years right after the war were the most difficult. This was caused by a serious lack of food in general. In order to fill hungry stomachs people's concern was concentrated on cereals, i.e. rice, but since rice was seriously in short supply it was compensated for by wheat flour (bread, noodles) and sweet potatoes.

b) The second stage came around the year 1955 when the rice supply became abundant. Consumption of sweet potatoes decreased sharply, and gradually cereals other than rice declined year after year.

c) The years after 1960 may be called the third stage. The importance of cereals generally in the Japanese diet has now reached an all-time low. The consumption of rice itself has been showing a gradual decrease over the last several years in spite of abundant harvests. Demand for rice is now virtually met by the available domestic supply.

During this period a significant change in consumer's attitudes towards bread, as well as towards other wheat flour products, seems to have occurred. Bread is no longer thought of merely as a second-best substitute for rice, but is being thought of as a staple food or *shushoku* in its own right.

[94]

Chapter Five. Seaweed or Bread for Breakfast?

EXHIBIT I

PER CAPITA FOOD CONSUMPTION PER DAY
—URBAN VS. RURAL—
(1971)

	CALORIES (unit)	PROTEIN (gram)	OIL & FATS (gram)	CARBOHYDRATES (gram)
Non-farm households				
Total intake	2,330	79.8	51.4	373
Vegetable origin	1,913	43.1	28.2	360
Cereals	1,218	23.8	4.2	262
Sugar	75	—	—	19
Confectionery	124	2.1	2.1	24
Oil & fats	145	0.2	16.2	—
Vegetables	81	4.8	0.5	15
Fruits	59	1.0	0.4	14
Pulses, potatoes	121	8.1	3.5	15
Animal origin	398	36.4	22.9	10
Fish, shellfish	114	18.2	3.5	2
Meat	139	9.2	11.1	—
Eggs	70	5.7	5.0	—
Milk & dairy products	75	3.3	3.3	8
Farm households				
Total intake	2,320	75.7	41.4	396
Vegetable origin	2,002	45.2	25.4	386
Cereals	1,337	25.6	4.2	295
Sugar	74	—	—	19
Confectionery	122	2.1	2.1	24
Oil & fats	119	0.2	13.2	—
Vegetables	75	4.6	0.5	14
Fruit	40	0.6	0.4	9
Pulses, potatoes	133	8.8	3.9	17
Animal origin	303	30.3	16.0	7
Fish, shellfish	117	17.9	3.5	2
Meat	79	5.4	6.1	—
Eggs	60	4.9	4.3	—
Milk & dairy products	48	2.1	2.1	2

Source: *Kokumin Eiyō Chōsa Seiseki 1971* ('Results of National Nutrition Survey'), Tokyo: Ministry of Health & Welfare, 1972.

This trend has been part of a broader movement, away from traditional Japanese-style food to a mixture of Japanese-style and western-style food, which gained momentum during the late fifties as people became more conscious about nutrition and a healthful, well-balanced diet and as consumers' standard of living improved. Now the Japanese cereal diet consists of a combination of rice and bread as well as noodle-type products.

The Japanese use of foods other than staple cereals has increased considerably over the last 15 years. Among them, sugar has more than doubled, fats and oil increased some 4 times, and pulses by some 11%. Food items of animal origin increased by nearly $1\frac{1}{2}$ times. In this category, meat increased some 3.7 times, eggs 3 times, dairy products 4.4 times. The increase of dairy products and meat especially may be related to some extent to the spread of the bread-eating habit as a regular part of the Japanese daily diet.

This improvement in the quantity and quality of Japanese dietary items in a short period of time may be caused by changes in general attitude towards diet, spread of knowledge of nutrition, general westernization of Japanese daily life, and increases in personal and family income. However, there is still a considerable difference in food consumption between urban and rural households. Exhibit 1 compares nutrient intake from main food items for farm households versus that for non-farm households and points up the greater importance of cereals and the lower consumption of meat and dairy products in farm households.

The future of Japanese dietary habits will see a further improvement in the standard of basic nutrition and further westernization in the choice of foods. Along with these changes, demand for more animal-origin foods, such as meat and dairy products, will be expected to increase further, as well as the development of new foods such as convenience versions or frozen foods.

At the same time, it should *not* be expected that the Japanese diet of the future will closely resemble that of the United States or western Europe. Despite the incorporation of many features of

Chapter Five. Seaweed or Bread for Breakfast?

western origin, the Japanese diet will continue to be more heavily weighted towards carbohydrate consumption than the U.S. diet, and the basic Japanese menu will continue to be rice-oriented for many years to come although the absolute volume intake is decreasing.

Kitchen facilities and cooking methods

ONE characteristic of Japanese houses after the Second World War has been a flood of modern electrical appliances. Sewing machines, electric washing machines, vacuum cleaners are in general use, and television sets are in almost every home. On the other hand, though improvements are of course being seen, in many cases the homes are lacking in basic amenities, such as flush toilets, baths, or running hot water, and are small and crowded to live in.

The kitchen is no exception. The ownership rate of electric refrigerators is very high (91.6%), and sophisticated appliances such as dish washers and even electronic microwave ovens have been introduced into the market. However, average Japanese kitchens are still somewhat behind western kitchens in terms of the equipment westerners consider essential; the ownership of conventional cookers, ovens, stainless steel sinks, ventilation fans, hot water heaters, etc. is still rather low. (Exhibit 2.)

EXHIBIT 2
OWNERSHIP OF KITCHEN FACILITIES
(FEBRUARY 1972)

	HOUSEHOLDS		
	ALL	RURAL	URBAN
Electric refrigerator	91.6%	87.8%	93.5%
Gas range (1966)	28	14	34
Stainless sink	56.9	48.1	60.5
Hot water heater (gas)	50.4	34.2	56.4
Ventilation fan	39.1	24.7	45.0
Electric rice cooker (1965)	50.9	35.4	57.6

Source: *Shōhi to Chochiku no Dōkō 1970* ('Trends of Consumption and Savings'), Tokyo: Economic Planning Agency, 1972, pp. 118–120.

[97]

Probably the most important of the household appliances from the housewife's point of view has been the automatic rice cooker, first electric and more recently gas. The old method of preparing rice required a longer cooking time and continued attention while on the fire. The electric or gas cookers come with switches that turn on and off automatically and with thermostat controls, thus allowing the housewife to sleep later in the morning or to leave the house while the rice is cooking.

To some extent the disadvantages of the kitchen are those of the Japanese urban home in general, in particular shortage of space. This means that storage space is at a premium; and even though refrigerators are usually small by American standards there is sometimes no room to put them in the kitchen and they have to be put in the living area. However, the modern homes that are being built, such as the government *danchi* apartments, while still very limited in space, have more carefully planned kitchen areas, and no doubt the future will see as much ingenuity being applied to the problem of efficient overall kitchen design in Japan as has up to now been given to the design of individual appliances.

The difference in kitchen facilities may be partly due to the difference in cooking methods between western countries and Japan. For instance, in the preparation of a traditional Japanese meal, fire is used less than in western countries. The only dishes which require heating for a given meal might be rice, soup, and one other dish containing meat or fish; other dishes might be raw cucumber or seaweed, pickles *(su-no-mono)*, and *tsukudani* (preserved fish or vegetables boiled with soy sauce), which need no heating. Accordingly, most Japanese housewives are able to make do on two (or even one) gas or electric rings.

There are few Japanese recipes which require heating for a long time like stew, and the basic soups *(misoshiru, sumashijiru)* are prepared very quickly. Besides, the quantity of meat, fish, or vegetables eaten at a time is considerably smaller than in most western countries, and the meat is often cut into thin slices before cooking.

[98]

Chapter Five. Seaweed or Bread for Breakfast?

Usually little oil is used in cooking except for *tempura* (deep-fried fish and vegetables).

One distinguishing difference in heating food is in the use of the oven, which is not an item of traditional Japanese cooking equipment; most Japanese housewives do not think an oven is necessary to their cooking even when they prepare western-style food, and oven ownership is very low. Microwave ovens are unlikely to change this fact, especially because suitable pre-prepared food is not yet being marketed in Japan.

Another general point in which Japanese cooking differs from western cooking is in taste. On the average, Japanese dishes have stronger tastes, seasoned mainly with soy sauce, because they always accompany rice, which is very bland. One other point may be that the Japanese use spices very sparingly. Most of them use white pepper, however, and they use it in almost every meat dish they prepare regardless of kind of meat or cooking method.

It is often said that Japanese place more importance on the look of dishes than westerners do, for in the West taste is said to be more important than appearance. The Japanese housewife is much concerned about the color and shape of food she prepares and uses a wide variety of plates and bowls in one meal, and in the table setting puts plates and bowls around the rice bowl.

Chopsticks have traditionally been the only eating utensil used for Japanese meals. The spoon is used frequently, particularly for small children and for some types of dishes (western-style soup, curried rice, etc.) in recent times. Knives and forks, on the other hand, are still not used extensively in Japanese homes. Forks in particular are not commonly used.

What's on the menu?

Bruno Taut was able to write in 1936 that the doors of a Japanese house are generally 5 ft. 8½ ins. high and thus "adequate for the average height of a Japanese". At the same time he quoted a

Japanese scientist of the time as finding that the "small size of the Japanese is no peculiarity of race, but a consequence of their style of living, their food and customs."

The standard height of a traditionally styled Japanese door is still around 5 ft. 8 ins. American businessmen usually tower several inches above their Japanese counterparts. But at the same time diet improvements and a more westernized and upright style of living are resulting in a younger generation of Japanese who themselves are significantly taller at 15 than their own fathers and mothers. The average (modal) height for Japanese adult males aged 20 in 1950 was 161.5 cm and in 1971, 165.9 cm; for those aged 70 and more it was 154.3 and 155.7 respectively.[2] Many Japanese now have to duck as they walk through doors; school desks no longer fit the age-group to which they are allocated; bus-seats cramp the legs of most Japanese men under 25.

Certainly the Japanese diet is more nourishing now than 35 years ago and awareness of nutrition considerations much more highly developed. Dietetics are incorporated into the curriculum of high school home economics courses, and many girls attend cooking schools before they get married. One well-known cooking magazine *Eiyō to Ryōri* ('Nutrition and Food') is full of menu suggestions that stress the need for a balanced diet.

Over a fifteen-year period, there have been big increases in per capita consumption of animal-origin protein (averaging 43.5 grams per day in 1971, compared with 22.1 grams in 1953) and of oil and fats (up from 20.1 grams to 48.7 grams).[3] The importance of carbohydrates has decreased, if slowly, over the same period.

Compared with developed countries in the West, however, the Japanese diet is still inferior in terms of average daily calorie intake (2,471 in 1970 compared with 3,290 in the U.S.A., 3,180 in

[2] *1971 Kokumin Eiyō Chōsa Seiseki* ('Preliminary Report on the National Nutrition Survey'), Tokyo: Ministry of Health and Welfare, 1972, p. 59.

[3] *Ibid.*, p. 9.

Chapter Five. Seaweed or Bread for Breakfast?

Britain and 2,940 in Germany).[4] A far smaller percentage of daily calories are of animal origin (13%) than in countries like the U.S.A. (34%), Britain (31%), or W. Germany (28%), though in this respect Japan is not too dissimilar to Italy (17%). In particular, the typical Japanese diet is deficient in most vitamins; vitamin preparations are accordingly big business, and if you switch on one of the commercial TV channels, the odds are that it will not be long before you are exposed to a commercial for a vitamin pill, drink, lozenge, or ampoule.

So though a decreasing Engel's coefficient is usually thought to be a mark of development, many Japanese households would be better advised to reverse this trend and to increase their expenditures on food with high nutritional value.

The most important feature of the Japanese diet is that it centers around rice (or a substitute for rice), other dishes being considered as supplementary items. In fact, the word *shushoku* or "main food" is commonly used to describe rice and its substitutes, such as noodles, bread, or other cereal products. Although the current trend is in the direction of decreased intake of *shushoku*, most Japanese still consider several bowls of boiled rice as the center of any meal. All the other dishes are called collectively *okazu* or *fukushoku*, literally meaning "subsidiary food" or "side-dishes". And as has been often pointed out, the word *gohan* means both rice and food in general.

New food products are taken into the Japanese housewife's menu-planning in accordance with this context. Bread is considered to be a substitute for rice and, as such, it is now consumed in a sizeable number of Japanese homes. Most other types of new foods introduced into the Japanese diet fall into the category of *okazu*, to supplement the central dish of rice.

Thus to a Japanese, meat, fish, and vegetables are all in the *okazu* category, whether the products are western or Japanese in origin.

---

[4] *Nihon Kokusei Zue 1972* ('Charted Survey of Japan'), Tokyo: Tsuneta Yano Kinenkai, 1972, pp. 123–124. Figures based on FAO Annual Book.

This contrasts with the way of thinking in most western countries, which are "course-oriented"; in other words the meal is built up of courses, one of which (usually the meat course) would be considered the "main course". This approach could be described diagrammatically as a linear approach to menu-planning, while the Japanese approach is basically circular, with the bowl of rice—to elaborate on this idea—in the center and the *okazu* round the circumference.

The Japanese have so far remained addicted to white polished rice despite various attempts to encourage consumption of the more nutritious brown rice; after the war there was a thriving black-market in white rice since only brown rice and other cereals were available through the regular government-controlled rationing channels. Two or more bowls of rice having traditionally been the main body of each meal, accompanied by other side dishes, the typical Japanese diet tends to be quite substantial in volume and weight, if not in nutritional value. A Japanese expects to *feel* full after a meal. Thus the most important reason given for not using bread rather than rice for breakfast, and a frequent complaint made about bread or ready-to-eat cereals such as corn flakes, is usually that they are not "substantial enough", or that they "don't make one feel satisfied."

The traditional Japanese breakfast has always been one of the foreign traveler's least favorite experiences in Japan, and few foreigners, even after years in Japan, can really speak with enthusiasm of this meal. Most Japanese people still eat rice, accompanied by beanpaste soup *(misoshiru)*, pickles, seaweed dipped in soy sauce, green tea, maybe a raw egg, and from time to time a piece of cooked but cold fish. At the same time, a new tradition of a bread-oriented breakfast is now firmly established in Japan, especially among white-collar workers' families. This usually consists of toasted white bread and black tea or instant coffee. Some homes serve both types of breakfast, rice to some members of the family and bread to others. People often switch from one to the other, having rice some days and bread on other days. Children usually eat bread more often than rice from the age of about 5 up.

Only a few households regularly serve corn flakes and other ready-to-eat cereals. Since their introduction in 1964, they have been marketed more successfully as a between-meals confectionery or snack item than as a breakfast food.

It is not customary for Japanese to drink alcoholic beverages while eating the main dish of the meal, rice or noodles. *Sake*, traditional Japanese rice wine, or beer is often served and drunk at the same time as side dishes are eaten, and many small food dishes may be served as an accompaniment to drinks in a formal dinner party or to drinks served in an establishment outside the home. People seldom take any alcohol at or before lunch.

Green tea, a traditional Japanese beverage, is served after almost all meals and may be served during the meal. Other types of beverage are not considered appropriate to serve at a meal, but serving instant coffee or tea ("black tea") after meals is now becoming popular.

BREAD

BREAD has been known in Japan for many years; it is said to have first been introduced from Europe in 1486. However, only in the late 19th century was it marketed on any scale in the country. Prof. B. H. Chamberlain, writing in 1891, was able to report that recent statistics showed that bread-eating was on the wane, having been the "rage among the lowest class in 1890"! Its real growth, however, has occurred only since World War II. As already noted, from 1949–1955 production of bread increased rapidly as a substitute for rice; Japan had lost her two main sources of rice supply, Taiwan and Korea, and in the years after the war there was in any case a serious deficiency in rice supply. However, bread at this stage was regarded as a second-best substitute for rice, and when the rice supply increased from 1955, bread production drifted back, through 1959. Even in 1959, however, bread production remained higher than in any year before 1954. By the end of the fifties, it is thought that consumers were beginning to think of bread as a valuable *shushoku* or staple cereal in its own right, with a growing number of consumers combining, from choice, both bread and rice in their daily diet. The Japanese bread supply has increased especially in the past three years (Exhibit 3).

EXHIBIT 3
PRODUCTION OF FLOUR AND RICE
(1955–1971)

	THOUSAND TONS	FLOUR INDEX 1955= 100	% CHANGE FROM PREVIOUS YEAR	THOUSAND TONS	RICE INDEX 1955= 100	% CHANGE FROM PREVIOUS YEAR
1955	754	100	+ 1	12,385	100	+36
1956	723	96	− 4	10,899	88	− 2
1957	673	89	− 7	11,464	93	+ 5
1958	656	87	− 3	11,993	97	+ 5
1959	632	84	− 4	12,501	101	+ 4
1960	628	83	− 1	12,858	104	+ 3
1961	660	88	+ 5	12,419	100	− 3
1962	690	92	+ 5	13,009	105	+ 5
1963	716	95	+ 4	12,812	103	− 2
1964	760	100	+ 6	12,584	102	− 2
1965	865	115	+14	12,409	100	− 1
1966	893	118	+ 3	12,745	103	+ 3
1967	897	119	+ 1	14,453	117	+13
1968	944	125	+ 5	14,449	116	0
1969	979	130	+ 4	14,003	113	− 3
1970	970	129	− 1	12,689	102	− 9
1971	952	126	− 2	10,887	88	−14

Sources: Flour: 1955–1969, *Shokuryō Kanri Tōkei Nempō 1968* ('Statistical Yearbook of Foodstuffs Administration'), Tokyo: Shokuryō-cho, 1969, p. 341; 1970 and 1971, *Pan News*, July 3, 1972.
Rice: *Sakumotsu Tōkei* ('Crop Statistics'), Tokyo: Nōrin Tōkei Kyōkai, 1972, p. 173.

Chapter Five. Seaweed or Bread for Breakfast?

Bread statistics include three categories of products:

a) *White bread* by definition is relatively unsweetened, mainly sold in loaves or as table rolls. A small loaf (130–170 g) of white bread generally retails at around ¥60 in Tokyo, somewhat more outside Tokyo. It is often sold pre-sliced and pre-wrapped by the retailer. White bread accounted for almost half of total bread consumption by weight in 1971.

b) *Buns* are by definition sweetened bread, mainly sold in bun-shape. They include buns filled with jam, cream, bean-jam, etc., and other types of sweetened rolls.

c) *Other* includes special types of bread, such as rye bread or bran bread.

White bread is eaten most often at breakfast time, especially toasted, with butter. Jam is often eaten with it, but there is little use of other spreads. It is thought that children eat more bread than adults. What is not known, of course, is the extent to which today's children will drop or retain the bread-eating habit as they become adults. One point of importance is the fact that young children are being conditioned to accept bread as a regular part of the daily diet *outside* as well as inside the home, through the school-feeding program. In most primary schools (ages 6–11), complete meals are provided for the children, with bread rather than rice as the staple cereal.

FISH

FISH is a major source of animal-origin protein for the Japanese. In 1971 more than half of the Japanese per capita animal-origin protein intake per day (in terms of weight) was from fish. It is not surprising therefore that Japan continues to occupy a high place among the fishing nations of the world.

In Japan, a wider variety of fish and shellfish are eaten than in America or Europe. People buy fish at neighborhood fish shops in sufficient quantity for one meal. Dried fish is also very popular, but canned fish is not as commonly used. Usually fish dishes are served at supper, but sometimes dried fish is served at breakfast with rice and soup. Some of the kinds of fish popularly eaten are tuna, mackerel, horse-mackerel, salmon, mackerel-pike, codfish, flatfish, cuttlefish, octopus, etc. Tuna, flatfish, and cuttlefish are often eaten raw *(sashimi* and *sushi)*, and horse-mackerel, mackerel-pike, and sardines are often eaten in dried form. In the household, cooking methods of fish are relatively simple; representative recipes are *shioyaki* (fish broiled & seasoned with salt only), *nitsuke* (fish stewed and seasoned with soy sauce, sugar, salt, and *sake*), and *agemono* (fried fish with or without coating).

MEAT

TOTAL demand of meat in Japan has shown remarkable increase year by year. The annual intake per capita was 8.5 kg in 1964 and 18.6 kg in 1971.[5] However, as compared with foreign countries, the level of meat consumption in Japan is still very low: the corresponding figures for 1968/69 were 109 kg in the United States, 83 kg in France, 75 kg in U.K., and 73 kg in Germany. Consequently it is believed that the demand for meat in Japan will increase still further.

Pork and chicken, particularly broilers, have shown a striking increase. Chicken accounted for only 13% of total Japanese supply in 1955, with pork 33% and beef 46%. By 1971 the share of chicken had increased to 29%, with pork 45% and beef 17%.[6] In 1966 chicken became the second most important meat after pork. This increase of chicken and pork and the corresponding decrease of beef is due at least partly to the fact that the raising of chicken and pork does not require as much land space as beef.

Some years back, the government estimated that the Japanese

[5] *Nōrin Suisan Tōkei 1972* ('Agriculture, Forestry and Fisheries Production Statistics'), Tokyo: Nōrin Tōkei Kyōkai, 1972, p. 68.
[6] *Ibid.*, p. 259.

demand for meat per person per year would reach 14 to 16 kg in 1976; this would generate a national total demand of 1,990,000 to 2,320,000 metric tons, 2.4 to 2.8 times the 1964 figure. This estimated goal was already attained in 1971, five years prior to the originally estimated date. It is therefore obvious that Japanese domestic meat production will never fulfill the demand in the years to come, and Japan will have to depend on import. It is thought that the share of beef will decrease still further, with corresponding increases in the shares of chicken and pork.

With respect to the use of meat, it is well to recall its normal role in Japan as one of the side-dishes to rice and not as the main focal point of a meal. The actual quantity of meat eaten per person, when it is on the household menu, is much smaller than in an equivalent American home. Its high cost means that it remains a luxury item for most homes; even when it is served, the bulk of the meal is supplied by rice.

Beef is usually bought raw by weight, cut into thin slices. Its price in recent years has increased rapidly. It is almost twice as high as chicken, mainly because of the absolute shortage of supply compared with potential demand. Good quality beef for *sukiyaki* costs around ¥250 for 100 grams, but the price would of course be lower for dishes using less tasty cuts.

The best-known Japanese beef dish is *sukiyaki* (hot-pot of beef with vegetables and soy sauce seasoning). Beef steak *(bifu-teki* in Japanese) is also a very popular dish, but owing to the recent price hike of beef not many people are able to include beef steak in everyday menu-planning. Other popular dishes of beef include *batayaki* (beef grilled with butter in a pan) and *tsukeyaki* (beef soaked in a mixed sauce of soy sauce, *sake*, seasonings, etc., and grilled).

Like other meat, pork is also usually sold cut in slices and bought by weight. The price of pork has tended to fluctuate in recent years but is somewhat cheaper than beef on average. The price at present ranges from ¥80 to ¥150 per 100 grams for the most usually consumed cuts.

Pork is used more often in Japanese daily meals than beef. The most popular dish of pork is probably *tonkatsu* (deep fried pork). In addition *shōga-yaki* (pork marinated in a mixed sauce of soy sauce, grated ginger root and other seasoning), pork chops, and *yakibuta* (roast pork in Chinese style) are also popular dishes. Stewed pork in curry sauce with vegetables, served with rice, is an especially popular dish among children; beef and chicken are also used for this dish, but for home cooking, pork is most common.

Chicken is usually bought raw by weight, the birds being cut into pieces without bone and differentiated by grade, rather than by parts (leg, breast, etc.). Recently, however, chickens have become more available by parts, with or without bone, or by the bird, with a growing popularity in broilers.

Many popular dishes of traditional Japanese style are made with chicken, including *oyako-domburi* (bowl of rice with chicken and egg on top), *chawan-mushi* (steamed egg-curd dissolved with soup, and mixed with chicken and vegetables), and *mizutaki* (hot-pot of chicken and vegetables boiled with soup). In addition, western-style chicken dishes such as fried and roast chicken are also popular. Omelettes, curry, and fried rice made with pieces of chicken and tomato ketchup and several Chinese-style dishes are also eaten in the home and in restaurants.

VEGETABLES AND FRUIT

THE relative importance of root vegetables such as radishes and turnips has been declining in Japan during recent years, while that of non-root vegetables has been increasing. It is interesting to note that some vegetables of western origin such as lettuce, celery, parsley, and Spanish paprika, which now appear separately in government statistics, did not do so before 1962. This suggests a trend towards the eating of raw vegetables more often than before.

Another event of recent development is indoor cultivation. The main crops from indoor cultivation are cucumbers, tomatoes, egg-plants, and Spanish paprika; constant supply of these vegetables is thus made possible all the year round at fairly stabilized prices. In weight terms, the leading vegetable is still the *daikon* or giant Japanese radish. This is followed by cabbage, onions, and cucumbers. Pulses are in a special category. They have been used for a long time as an important source of protein supply. Among various peas and beans, soybeans especially have been used widely as a food item, as edible oil, and as feed for animals. However, production of soybeans has decreased drastically; domestic production meets only 4% (1971) of the total soybeans demand, and 2,927,000 metric tons ($398,688,000) were imported from the U.S.A. and 283,000 metric tons ($39,214,000) from mainland China in 1971.[7]

Potatoes, especially sweet potatoes, were eaten by Japanese as an important substitute for rice in the years right after the war. However, the importance of the sweet potato as a food item has declined: it is now used primarily for the production of starch. Sweet potato harvests have been decreasing year after year over the last ten years. Production of white potatoes has been relatively static in the same ten years. The main uses of white potatoes are, in order of importance, as starch, as food, and as fodder.

Virtually all vegetables consumed are bought raw, dried, or pickled. Frozen and canned versions are not widely used.

The production of fruit in 1970 amounted to 6,537,000 metric tons in volume terms,[8] which doubled the production of ten years before. Fruit culture was once regarded as one of the high-growth industries, but the recent labor shortage in farm households and rapid increase of wages caused the cost of fruit production to increase, and it is no longer considered as profitable a business as it once was. The area of fruit cultivation in general has been declining over the past few years, and since the consumption of

[7] *Nihon Bōeki Geppō, Dec. 1971* ('Japan Exports & Imports, Monthly Report'), Tokyo: Ministry of Finance, p. 54.

[8] *Nōrin Suisan Tōkei Geppō, April 1972* ('Agriculture, Forestry and Fisheries Production Statistics, Monthly Report'), Tokyo: Ministry of Agriculture and Forestry, 1972, p. 26.

fruit is growing quickly it is expected that supply will not meet demand in the ten years ahead. The main fruits Japan produces are tangerines and apples, followed by persimmons, Japanese pears, and peaches. Since prices of domestically produced fruit are generally high, Japanese fruit is hardly competitive in the international market except for tangerines and apples. On the other hand, Japan has to depend entirely on imports for bananas, lemons, and pineapples, for which the demand is ever increasing. Banana imports were liberalized in 1963, lemons in 1964, and grapefruit in 1971, but oranges are still under restriction.

DAIRY PRODUCTS

THE expansion of the Japanese consumption of dairy products in recent years has been spectacular. Substantial increases have occurred in the production of fresh milk, especially for drinking straight, of powdered milk, skimmed milk, butter and cheese. (Exhibit 4.) About two-thirds of the Japanese homes in the main metropolitan areas have milk delivered daily, mainly for drinking plain, but the average quantity is low; it is usually sold in glass bottles containing 180 cc or 200 cc (0.38–0.43 U.S. pints), and the average daily order is only two bottles. In addition, milk is widely available through milk-stands in railroad stations, department stores, etc., with fruit flavors popular. Cost for home delivery ranges from ¥30–¥35 per bottle.

One of the most interesting sectors of the dairy product market has been that of cheese. Before and immediately after the war, consumption was on a very limited scale. Although by 1950 production had recovered to the prewar level, it was only in the following years that the market began to expand: 5,213 metric tons in 1960, 33,194 in 1968, and 42,906 in 1971.[9] Processed rather than fresh cheese has been responsible for the growth of its category;

[9] *Shokuryō Nenkan 1972* ('Foodstuffs Yearbook'), Tokyo: Nihon Shokuryō Shinbun-sha, 1972, p. 197.

EXHIBIT 4
ANNUAL DOMESTIC PRODUCTION
OF FRESH MILK AND DAIRY PRODUCTS
(1960, 1966, 1968, 1971)

UNIT: metric tons (1)

	1960	1966	1968	1971
Fresh milk total	1,887	3,417	4,013	4,761
for straight drinking	987	1,972	2,323	2,623
for processing	742	1,251	1,504	2,138
Sweetened condensed milk	42,824	31,278	37,353	42,081
Evaporated milk	6,175	7,520	6,529	6,763
Whole powdered milk	7,398	27,608	27,492	36,381
Sweetened powdered milk	68	828	365	94
Adjusted powdered milk for babies	21,741	49,869	53,303	65,107
Sweetened condensed skim milk	24,720	23,357	n.a.	n.a.
Plain skim milk	10,552	26,391	n.a.	68,117
Ice cream mix powder	5,255	3,619	n.a.	6,478
Ice cream (2)	156	194	191	169
Butter	11,821	24,790	32,378	47,732
Cheese	5,213	26,611	33,194	42,906

Source: *Shokuryō Nenkan 1972* ('Foodstuffs Yearbook'), Tokyo: Shokuryō Shinbunsha, 1972, pp. 196, 197.

Notes: 1. Except fresh milk in thousand tons, and ice cream in thousand kl.

2. Includes only ice cream with 3% or more milk ingredient for Jan.–July 1971, and with 8% or more milk fat, 15% or more milk solids for August–December 1971, produced by factories with annual production capacity of 50 kl or more.

99% of all cheese sold is cheddar-based processed cheese. It is usually eaten in slices, either with bread or as an accompaniment to alcoholic drinks.

The price of cheese is high compared with that in other countries —usually ¥200 for a half-pound package. It is regarded as an extremely nutritious food item, and advertising sometimes claims in effect that it increases intelligence as well as strengthens the body.

It is true that Japanese per capita consumption of cheese remains very low compared with that of many other countries—only 409 grams in 1971—and the range of types consumed is very limited. However, cheese provides yet another example of the way in which a product which was previously scarcely consumed has entered into the consumption pattern of many Japanese homes.

SOUP PRODUCTS

THE Japanese have had a number of traditional soups of their own for many centuries, such as *misoshiru* (thick soup made by melting *miso* beanpaste in hot water) and *sumashijiru* (clear soup seasoned with soy sauce and salt). Those soups contain two or three vegetable ingredients and are served both at breakfast and supper (*sumashijiru* usually at supper only). The concept of soup in Japan differs somewhat from that in western countries in that soup is an important side dish rather than an appetizer. Western-style soup became part of the Japanese daily diet after the introduction of instant products, and it is accepted favorably as one variety of soup and drunk in the same manner as Japanese traditional soup.

The market for instant soup has been developed and enlarged at a considerable pace in the last several years owing to the westernization of Japanese diet habits. The estimated production in 1971 of the instant powdered version was reported as equivalent to 475 million servings. There are three varieties of instant soup on the Japanese market: powdered soup, condensed canned soup, and cubed bouillon. Among these, powdered soup has the largest share of the market and is heavily promoted by manufacturers; the recent expansion of the soup market is due mainly to the increase in this type of soup. Market leaders are Ajinomoto (KNORR), Nestlé (MAGGI), and Morinaga (MORINAGA), all powdered soups. KNORR is the largest with the widest range of varieties.

The Japanese market for condensed canned soup is still rather small compared with that for powdered soup and bouillon cubes, although in the past one to two years the import of canned soup has been rapidly increasing with an estimated 670 metric tons of import in 1971. Distribution is still far behind that of the powdered version and is not being supported by consumer promotions or advertising. Bouillon cubes have the longest history in the instant soup market, and they are used quite widely.

It is thought in the trade that there still remains a considerable latent demand in Japan for these western-style instant soups, and accordingly the market is expected to grow further. This development should not, however, be thought to mean an overall shift of consumption to western-style soup from traditional Japanese *misoshiru* or *sumashijiru*. The traditional types will still retain their popularity.

SOFT DRINKS

THE total Japanese market for soft drinks has greatly expanded. Production amounted to 614,478 kl in 1962, 1,699,000 kl in 1968, and 3,112,500 kl in 1971 (worth ¥403 billion at manufacturers' prices).[10]

The market is generally divided into three sections: carbonated, fruit juice, and lactic.

i) *Carbonated*

The growth of the soft drink market in Japan has been stimulated mainly by the carbonated drink sector; estimated production in 1971 was 2,313,500 kl as against 1,088,500 kl in 1968.[11] The growth of *cola* has been remarkable since free import of concentrate was allowed in 1960, and it now has over 40% of the carbonated sector in terms of volume, considerably more in terms of value. The heavily advertised COCA-COLA dominates. Although they are broken down separately, the divisions between *saida* ('cider'), *ramune*, and flavored carbonated drinks are rather arbitrary, the first two consisting of traditional carbonated drinks, and the last of newer products such as FANTA and MIRINDA. The tradi-

[10] *Ibid.*, p. 228.
[11] *Ibid.*

tional *saida* is holding its own against the American-style non-cola drinks, though these latter have expanded at a much faster rate.

ii) *Fruit drinks*

Several types of drink are included: *concentrated* drinks which are mixed with water before serving, containing 20–45% of fruit juice; *fruit-flavored bottled drinks* mostly un-carbonated, with a very low fruit juice content (but none-theless usually called *jūsu* in Japanese); and *canned fruit juice* of a high fruit juice content, 40% or over. Although it has remained sizable, the fruit drink sector has not expanded much. FANTA-type drinks, though also fruit-flavored, have been excluded from this category.

iii) *Lactic*

These drinks are made from skim milk fermented with lactic acid baccilli, sugar, and in some cases with fruit flavors. The leading brand, with a high proportion of the market, is CALPIS, which is almost a generic name for this type of product. The lactic concentrates have been con-sistently pushed as gift items at gift-giving seasons.

Soft drinks are of course extremely widely distributed, both for home and outside consumption; most are distributed by the traditional wholesaler/retailer system, though COCA-COLA and PEPSI use the franchised-bottlers'/direct delivery approach, which was a new system to Japan. Most retail outlets, even very small ones, that sell milk and other beverages have cooling equipment of some kind. Some of the competitors to soft drinks are mentioned in the paragraphs on tea and coffee which follow; other competition comes from milk, beer (increasing rapidly, with some brewers also active in soft drinks), and other alcoholic beverages. Plain water is univer-sally potable and widely consumed as a beverage.

Over half of total volume is thought to be accounted for by home consumption; makers of colas and the other non-carbonated drinks, which have tended to be more outside-home oriented than the market as a whole, have also tried to push home consumption with large bottle-sizes; most homes, as already noted, own refrigerators. Though soft drinks are of course heavily weighted towards summer consumption, the relative importance of the winter has increased, especially with respect to beer and ice cream.

TEA AND COFFEE

GREEN tea is the national beverage of Japan, where, it is said, it was first introduced in the 6th century, but it was not until the 18th century that it became a popular beverage for the general public. In Japan people drink green tea plain at all times of the day throughout the year, after, between, and sometimes during meals. Japan is one of the considerable tea-producing countries in the world, holding 7% of total world production. Almost 99% of the tea produced in Japan is directed to the manufacture of green tea; in 1970 the total production amounted to 91,200 metric tons.[12] However, in general, the production of tea shows no notable upward or downward trend in recent years.

The preparation of green tea is similar to that for black tea, i.e., pouring hot water on tea leaves in a teapot; it is simple and instantaneous. Only recently green-tea bags have been developed and marketed, but are still far from becoming popularized as compared with black-tea bags. Green-tea bags are mostly used in long distance railroad stations, where green tea in small plastic canisters is sold. One manufacturer is marketing freeze-dried powdered instant tea, but the product has not yet become a factor in the market (if, indeed, it ever will).

Black tea. Though far smaller than the market for green tea, the Japanese market for black tea, such as Indian or Ceylon, has more than doubled in the last several years. Consumption reached 6,200 metric tons in 1971 and in value terms was worth about

---

[12] *Nōrin Suisan Tōkei Geppō, April 1972, op. cit.,* p. 35.

¥12 billion. This growth was mainly achieved by the rapid expansion of tea bags following the introduction of automatic tea-bag packaging machines in 1963. Of the volume consumed in 1971, 44% was of tea bags. Leading tea brands are NITTOH and LIPTON, followed by BROOKE BOND. Since the import liberalization in 1971, branded foreign teas including TWININGS, RIDGWAY, MELROSE, etc. became abundantly available and are often used as gift items.

The "instant" black tea now on the Japanese market is mainly imported, but in very small volume. There are also on the market a small number of domestically developed instant black-tea brands which have a very marginal share of the market. Most of the domestically marketed products are tea powder with artificial lemon flavor and sugar added. Japan depends heavily on imports for the supply of black-tea leaves, the main countries of origin being Sri Lanka, U.K., India, and Taiwan.

Coffee. Until the introduction of instant coffee, coffee was a beverage consumed on a very small scale in Japan; it was considered a luxury beverage and mainly drunk outside the home. However, the aggressive marketing of instant coffee since 1961 has established coffee as a beverage for daily consumption in both city and rural households. The estimated Japanese supply of instant coffee totalled 15,500 tons in 1971, with a market value at the manufacturer's price of ¥34 billion. In the past five years, the market for instant coffee has grown twofold. The two international brands NESCAFÉ and MAXWELL together probably account for over 90% of the market, with NESCAFÉ the market leader. The most recent trend in the coffee market is the growth of regular coffee. Out of a total of 68,448 metric tons of coffee-bean imports in 1971, some 45% was directed to the production of regular roasted coffee.

CONFECTIONERY AND SNACK FOODS

THE Japanese market for confectionery and snack products is extremely difficult to define, owing to the wide range of items available. This observation is confirmed by the definitions of the

categories for which production information is available from
the Japan National Confectioners' Association. In addition, some
snack items for consumption with alcoholic beverages are not included, such as dried fish, smoked shell-fish, etc., nor are ready-to-
eat cereals, though part of their usage is accounted for by snack-type
consumption direct from the box.

Biscuits	—biscuits, crackers, and cookies
Cakes	—short-cake, pie, *castella* (sponge-cake), and others
Candy	—other candy, including nougat
Caramels	—both packaged and loose
Chewing gum	—sugar-coated, stick, bubble, and others
Chocolate	—both packaged and loose
Drops	—fruit and other drops
Japanese cakes	—*yōkan* (bean jelly), *manjū* (dumpling bun)
Japanese-type cookies	—sweet *sembei*, macaroons, rusks, wafers, and others
Rice crackers	—non-sweet *sembei, arare, okaki*, and other crackers made of rice
Others	—sugar-coated nuts, peanuts, raisins, dried peas and beans, sweetened peas, *karintō* (fried dough cake), and others.

In terms of value of production, the two leading Japanese categories in 1971 were chocolate and rice crackers, with production
at retail prices estimated to be worth ¥139 billion and ¥125 billion,
respectively. However, each category mentioned above had production worth ¥20 billion or more.

Two product categories, chocolate and chewing gum, have been
the market leaders in recent years in terms of rate of increase.
Chocolate production in value terms in 1971 (120,000 metric tons)
was five times the 1960 level (24,000 metric tons) with an especially
high rate of increase during the few years around 1967.[13] Chewing
gum grew dramatically up to about 1963, though its rise has been
more gradual since then; and the main chewing-gum manufacturer,

[13] *Seika Jihō*, May 1, 1972, Osaka: Shūkan Seika Jihō-sha.

LOTTE, has in fact diversified into the chocolate field. A conspicuous trend in the confectionery market for the past two to three years is that the consumers' desire for sweets has been decreasing, and nonsweet items like corn puffs, corn chips, potato chips, crackers, etc. are obtaining popularity as "snack food".

Receptivity to innovation

As will have been observed from the review above, for citizens of a homogeneous nation the Japanese are extremely adaptable and elastic in their national character and receptive to new things. Wide varieties of foods and dishes of western or Chinese origin are now an integral part of their regular menus, even though most of these foods and dishes were not introduced into Japan a century ago and many started developing only after World War II.

Purely Japanese traditional dishes are preferred by older people, whereas western or Chinese origin dishes are preferred by younger adults and children. This is partly because younger people have been more accustomed from their early childhood to the modern— that is, in most cases, western—foods which developed particularly after World War II, while older people were raised on the more traditional Japanese foods which were predominant earlier. A further factor contributing to this preference difference is that, while traditional Japanese foods are generally plain in taste, western or Chinese dishes are generally thicker in taste, or *aburakkoi* (literally "oily" or "greasy"). Believing it to be more nutritious, the Japanese have often fed their children on a more "modern" or "westernized" diet than they themselves can enjoy. The concept of "modern" is often blurred in Japan because "modern" means quite frequently "western", and not only in the food context. A further complication is that "westernization" does not usually mean the wholesale adoption of western methods, products, or culture, but rather an adaptation to fit into the Japanese context. Certain dishes of western origin have been so well adapted to the Japanese diet that they are no longer considered to be genuine western dishes (though they are not regarded as traditional dishes either). A good example is *tonkatsu*, deep-fried pork cutlet; this is now eaten with chopsticks rather than knife and fork, even though it is an adapted western-style dish.

Outside the broader question of westernization of diet, product format and package innovations are also, of course, features of current marketing. Quick acceptance of innovation in product format is exemplified by instant *rāmen* (Chinese noodles). The original form of this product, regular *rāmen*, has long been known, but it was consumed mostly outside the home, in Chinese restaurants. Instant versions have now made successful inroads into consumers' homes. Another example of this type is instant curry. Curried rice has been popular for many years, being eaten both at home and in restaurants, but it was previously prepared from curry powder. At present, most curried rice dishes served in the home are prepared from instant curry.

An example of quick acceptance of package innovation can be seen in mayonnaise and traditional condiments such as *shōyu* (soy sauce). Plastic squeeze bottles for mayonnaise, which previously was packed only in glass jars, have been accepted favorably by consumers. *Shōyu*, which was once available only in large glass bottles or bought in quantity from a shipping barrel, is widely available now in smaller plastic bottles. Some traditional Japanese pickles, normally produced in individual consumers' homes, are now available in commercially packaged forms at supermarkets and grocery stores.

Canned foods and frozen foods play only a minor role in the average Japanese consumer's diet, mainly because they are not compatible with the consumer's preference for fresh foods. However, there is increasing consumer acceptance of frozen foods owing to the spread of refrigerators with large freezer compartments. In fact, the demand for frozen foods by the general public increased seven times during the past four years, and the market for catering uses is even larger.

The Japanese pay high prices for the changes in their diet. The Economic Planning Agency stated that between 1965 and 1969, the rise in prices of agricultural products contributed 28% to the increase of consumer prices, and industrial foodstuff products another 14%.[14] Generally speaking, prices for agricultural products are substantially higher in Japan than in other major countries. (Exhibit 5.)

EXHIBIT 5

COMPARISON OF PRODUCERS' PRICES OF AGRICULTURAL PRODUCTS IN MAJOR COUNTRIES

(1968/1969 average)

UNIT: US$ per 100 kgs

	JAPAN	FRANCE	W. GERMANY	ITALY	UNITED KINGDOM	UNITED STATES
Wheat	15.4	8.76	9.76	10.76	6.43	4.56
Rice (powdered)	29.4	—	—	13.06	—	10.78
Barley	12.4	8.02	9.24	9.58	5.93	4.13
Beef	112.9	65.85	62.88	70.48	44.35	51.59
Pork	77.0	73.41	62.53	62.08	45.19	41.01
Poultry	57.3	75.17	48.00	139.21	38.58	31.53
Eggs	52.2	59.06	75.75	70.29	57.44	49.83
Fresh milk	12.9	8.42	10.10	10.82	8.56	11.57

Source: *Keizai Hakusho 1970* ('White Paper on the Economy'), Tokyo: Economic Planning Agency, 1970, p. 107.

Notes: 1. European statistics are from FAO "Prices of Agricultural Products and Fertilizers in Europe 1968/1969". Italian rice figures are based on FAO *Monthly Bulletin of Agricultural Economics and Statistics* (prices from June 1967 to May 1968).

2. U.S. figures are based on U.S. Department of Agriculture, *Agricultural Statistics 1969.*

3. Japan's figures are based on Ministry of Agriculture and Forestry, "Agricultural Village Price and Wage Survey."

[14] *Keizai Hakusho 1970* ('White Paper on the Economy'), Tokyo: Economic Planning Agency, 1970, p. 144.

Part III

MARKETING STRATEGY FOR JAPAN

CHAPTER SIX

Television Generation

JOSÉ M. DE VERA

TV ownership—TV and daily life—How people react to commercials

TV ownership

W HEN TV broadcasting started in Japan in 1953 there were 866 sets in the whole country; as of January 31, 1973, there were 14,740,469 color sets, but by February 28, 1973, they numbered 15,144,046, an increase of over 400,000. As of February 1972, there were in Japan 75.1 black-and-white and 61.1 color sets per 100 households. The total is still a staggering 136 sets per 100 households. The present spectacular diffusion has been explained in different ways by different people. Those obsessed with economic growth like to point out the coincidence of increase in TV sets with periods of booming economy. The first big jump in number of TV sets (908,710) took place in 1957, the year known among the Japanese as *Jinmu Keiki* to signify an economic prosperity not experienced since the days of Japan's first (and legendary) Emperor Jinmu. In spite of a tight money policy enforced by the government in the name of economic adjustment, the pace of consumption did not slow down. The year 1959 was considered even more prosperous than 1957 and people came to call it *Iwato Keiki*. It was about that time that the purchase of TV sets started to increase geometrically, 100,000 every two months, until in 1961 it reached the impressive figure of 10,000 sets per day.[1]

---

[1] Tōru Yamamoto, "The Growth of Television in Japan," *Studies of Broadcasting 1964*, Tokyo: The Nippon Hōsō Kyōkai, p. 122.

There is no point in denying the obvious parallel between the curve of TV ownership and the economic growth of Japan. The fact is, however, that most Japanese were eager to buy TV sets even when their incomes would not justify doing so. Right from the beginning, TV ownership was such a status symbol that cases were reported of families unable to buy a TV set who nevertheless bought antennas and installed them on top of their houses for public display! A new Japanese phrase was even coined, *TV kojiki* (TV beggars), for those who in order to watch TV made visiting rounds among the homes of their friends or relatives who owned sets. The initial eagerness was skillfully exploited by manufacturers, who installed TV sets in strategic places like railroad stations, public parks, and so on. In a Japan where urbanization has reached 72.2%[2] and crowds are omnipresent, it is not difficult to imagine the contagious enthusiasm generated around TV sets broadcasting *sumō* (Japanese wrestling) or the performances of favorite singers known before only by their voices. Allured by spectacle but annoyed by milling crowds and inclement weather, the Japanese took to buying TV sets at the sacrifice of other items that would have contributed more comfort or convenience to their daily lives. This Japanese phenomenon has puzzled many a sociologist and psychiatrist to the point of worried concern. "In domestic electrical appliances, including TV sets, Japan ranks among first-rate nations and in clothing among second-rate nations. But in environmental facilities, Japan is low among out-of-rank nations. Such is the unbalance between the three aspects of the Japanese people's life."[3]

In 1963, the Japanese government's Economic White Paper complained that "television sets . . . have been diffused at an abnormally high rate for the low standards of living of the Japanese,

---

[2] *1970 Population Census of Japan, Vol. I, Total Population,* Tokyo: Office of the Prime Minister, 1971.

[3] *White Paper on Living Standards 1967,* Tokyo: Economic Planning Agency, pp. 155–156.

with their poor diet and housing conditions."[4] This "abnormal" diffusion of TV sets appears clearly when we list the diffusion rates of durable goods in urban and rural areas. TV sets were more "important" than washing machines, electric cooking-pots for rice, fans, refrigerators, or vacuum cleaners. In both rural and urban milieus, TV tops the list. (Exhibit 1.)

EXHIBIT 1
DIFFUSION RATES OF DURABLE GOODS
(FEBRUARY 1972)

TV sets: black & white	75.1% (82.3% in 1971)
color	61.1
Electric washing machines	96.1
Electric fans	89.3
Radios	71.5
Electric refrigerators	91.6
Vacuum cleaners	79.8
Room coolers	9.3

Source: *Shōhi to Chochiku no Dōkō* ('Trends of Consumption and Savings'), Tokyo: Economic Planning Agency, 1972, *passim.*

In many Japanese families a TV set was the unanimous choice of what to buy first. Many homes have TV sets when they have no electric washing machines or vacuum cleaners. In other words, they prefer the TV set to labor-saving household devices. In absolute number of TV sets, Japan ranks second in the world, immediately after the U.S.A.

The diffusion of TV was conditioned but not caused by the economic growth of the country, for its priority among the Japanese lies beyond economic factors. Calling such a priority "unbalanced", one writer concluded that "in the present situation of this country a mature leisure situation is developed under immature conditions."[5] In 1969 a governmental White Paper on national living

---

[4] *Economic White Paper 1963*, Tokyo: Economic Planning Agency, p. 232.
[5] Tomoo Satō, "Sociological Structure of Mass Leisure", in *Studies on Broadcasting 1965*, Tokyo: The Nippon Hōsō Kyōkai, p. 110.

prepared by the Economic Planning Agency challenged the idea of a "mature leisure situation" in Japan. Measured against an American index of 100 for recreational facilities, the Japanese index was 7.7. When Japan was criticized for this incredibly low index despite being second in the world in ownership of TV sets, the Agency explained that the index was based solely upon the number of books per person in public libraries and area per person of city parks. The Japanese Finance Minister, asserting that the per capita national income of Japan will top America's by 1985, did not accept the figure of the Economic Planning Agency. The resulting controversy has pointed out once more the degree to which the Japanese leisure boom of mass media fame is centered around TV. In 1965 Japanese leisure hours for outdoor recreation were estimated at 457 per person as against 902 hours forecast for 1985 when, it is predicted, 5,000,000 hectares of forest and other natural facilities will be required for tourism alone.

Although Japan is a nation of almost 100% literacy and the Japanese are voracious readers (Japan publishes 500 million books a year, or 5 for every individual Japanese), TV is without dispute the top Japanese interest among leisure activities. According to a survey conducted in 1971, TV watching was the main leisure activity for 81.8% of the Japanese between 13 and 69 years of age. The nearest rival to TV, newspaper reading, was 49.7 percent. No other leisure activity (not even "conversation" or "women's talk" among wives) is comparable to TV watching. This fact is more impressive in view of the leisure boom—the *bakansu* boom—that has descended upon the country. For instance, there are in Japan an estimated 2 million pinball *(pachinko)* machines in 30,000 parlors. But only 10.0% of the Japanese refer to it as a main leisure activity. The curve of "TV addiction" follows the international pattern. It is high among teen-agers (84.2% of males and 84.0% of females between 13 and 19 years of age), declines in the twenties and thirties, and reaches a new peak (86.7% among males, 87.7% among females) in the fifties. (Exhibit 2.)

EXHIBIT 2

HOW JAPANESE PEOPLE SPEND THEIR LEISURE TIME
(1971)

	ALL	FARMERS	PRIVATE BUSINESS OWNERS	LARGE-SIZE ENTERPRISE WHITE-COLLAR WORKERS	SMALL AND MEDIUM-SIZE ENTERPRISE WHITE-COLLAR WORKERS	LARGE-SIZE ENTERPRISE BLUE-COLLAR WORKERS	SMALL AND MEDIUM-SIZE ENTERPRISE BLUE-COLLAR WORKERS	FAMILY EMPLOYEES	SCHOOL CHILDREN, STUDENTS	UNEMPLOYED
Number of respondents (100%)	(2589)	(219)	(234)	(187)	(160)	(211)	(443)	(567)	(375)	(124)
Sitting at home	33.5%	39.7%	34.6%	38.5%	37.5%	34.1%	33.0%	38.6%	17.1%	34.7%
Rest	28.9	26.9	25.2	32.6	35.0	40.8	27.8	17.1	39.2	29.8
Conversation with friends	24.3	33.3	23.1	12.3	22.5	19.4	21.7	33.2	20.3	27.4
Writing or telephoning friends	10.0	7.3	4.7	8.0	16.3	10.9	8.4	11.6	13.3	8.1
Watching TV	81.8	85.4	82.5	80.2	73.8	86.3	82.6	78.5	84.3	82.3
Listening to radio	18.6	10.0	12.4	17.6	20.6	20.4	15.1	13.9	41.6	7.3
Listening to records	15.3	5.5	9.0–	19.8	26.3	19.0	15.1	7.8	30.4	8.9
Motion pictures	5.7	3.2	4.3	8.6	9.4	6.2	7.2	1.6	10.9	0.8
Reading newspapers	49.7	52.1	60.7	60.4	52.5	55.9	46.3	53.1	29.9	42.7
Reading magazines	23.7	14.6	18.4	20.9	30.0	25.1	20.8	22.2	35.2	21.8
Reading books	18.8	7.3	9.8	40.6	29.4	23.7	9.9	14.5	29.1	14.5
Keeping a diary	7.0	15.5	5.1	3.2	6.9	7.6	5.4	7.9	6.4	4.0
Practical study (English conversation, etc.)	2.9	0.5	1.3	7.0	3.1	1.9	1.1	1.8	7.7	2.4

Source: *Zenkoku Ikō Chōsa Kekka-hyō—Seikatsu no naka no TV* ('Result of a Survey on National Trends—TV in Daily Life'), Tokyo: NHK Public Opinion Culture Institute, November 1971, p. 79.

A survey conducted in June of 1969 showed that 91% of the Japanese come in daily contact with TV. A similar survey in 1968 showed that 84% come in daily contact with TV, 75% read newspapers, and 11% listen to radio. Six years before, only 35% of the Japanese watched TV daily as against 57% who listened to the radio every day. Japanese moviegoers keep decreasing in alarming numbers: in 1958 the tickets sold reached a peak of 1,100 million; in 1964 the tickets sold were 431,000,000. During the fiscal year 1965–1966 no fewer than 666 movie theaters in the country closed down, leaving a total of 5,153 to serve ever dwindling audiences.[6] The expression *Sanshu no Jingi* refers to the sacred treasures of the Imperial Family, the sword, the mirror, and the jewel. But in recent years it has come to mean rather disrespectfully the three "musts" in electric appliances: washing machine, refrigerator, and TV. As the diffusion of these items reached a point near saturation, the *Sanshu no Jingi* changed into automobile, air conditioner, and again television. But this time it was color television. The initial impetus of the Japanese towards the purchase of TV sets found a further stimulus (or was it justification?) in two events of extraordinary national importance: one took place in 1959 and the other in 1964. The foreign reader may have some difficulty in grasping the importance of these two events because both spring from deep-seated roots in Japanese character.

The first event was the wedding of the Crown Prince. The choice of the bride was surrounded by secrecy and discretion. The major newspapers pledged to refrain from speculations and at a given day and hour they launched an extraordinary issue with the name and picture of the bride, who was a commoner. It was the first time in the history of Japan that a future emperor was to marry a girl outside the narrow circles of the nobility. The initial surprise gave way very soon to sheer delight and enthusiasm. The Crown Prince had

---

[6] Uni Japan Film, *Japanese Films 1969*, Tokyo: Association for the Diffusion of Japanese Films Abroad, pp. 61–62.

never appeared to the people as especially bright or appealing. But now the details of how his courage and decision had won the battle against court pressure that at first frowned upon a commoner were widely spread. On the other hand, the beauty, simplicity, intelligence, and modesty displayed by the bride-to-be won the heart of the whole nation. The young generation, trying to disentangle itself from traditional forms of pre-arranged marriages, took the marriage as a symbol of its own aspirations; democrats interpreted it as a step forward in the march of the country towards democratization; housewives found it as romantic as a soap-opera; businessmen thought it was ominous that the Imperial Family would be related to industrialists; Catholics were elated by the fact that the girl had attended the University of the Sacred Heart. There was scarcely a segment of the population that remained indifferent to the event. In this atmosphere of expectation and national interest the Imperial Household announced that the ceremony would include a colorful parade through the streets of Tokyo. Immediately the Japan Broadcasting Corporation announced that it would cover the whole ceremony via 108 TV cameras; and on April 1, 1959, eight TV stations started broadcasting, in time for the national event. For the first time, the man in the street would be able to witness the ancient rite by which the unbroken line of the Japanese Imperial Family has been maintained through the centuries. In spite of growing popular coldness towards the emperor-system, curiosity, coupled with sympathy for the young bride and groom, was a powerful stimulus for Japanese to attend the ceremony in one form or another. This stimulus was reflected in the 2,166,304 TV sets which were sold. While the number of sets in 1958 was 1,982,379 (or 11.0% of the households), in 1959 the total number grew to 4,148,683 (or 23.1% of the households).

The second event that increased the role of television in Japan was the Olympic Games in Tokyo in 1964. Perhaps no other nation in the world is more concerned than Japan with the impression she makes on foreigners. A foreigner can hardly exchange a few phrases with a Japanese before he is confronted with the ritualistic question: "How do you like Japan?" To the dismay of non-Japanese viewers of TV, when the foreign athletes participating in the Universiade Games in Tokyo (1968) were leaving the stadium in the closing ceremony, they were surrounded by Japanese radio and TV interviewers more interested in knowing what they thought of Mount Fuji, Japanese girls, and the accommodations they were provided than in the results of the competition. Similarly, the Japanese saw in the Olympic Games of 1964 a unique occasion through which to measure themselves against the West, to show to the West their achievements in technology and economy, to improve their image in the eyes of the world, and to mend fences that they themselves broke through years of war. From 13,378,773 in 1963 the number of TV sets in Japan jumped to 15,662,921 in 1964. In 1969 the launching of Apollo 11 very much stimulated the sale of color TV sets. Newspapers reported frantic telephone calls from shopowners pleading with the manufacturers to send more sets on the eve of the lunar adventure. Today about 75.1 B/W and 61.1 color sets per 100 households are in use.

TV and daily life

TELEVISION plays a definite role in Japanese daily life. A survey conducted in 1966 found that the average time spent daily for TV-viewing by the general population of Tokyo was three hours and six minutes; as a separate group, women averaged three hours and 42 minutes; more than 50% of the Tokyo population consider themselves assiduous viewers and only eight percent consider themselves sporadic viewers.[7] For the purpose of that particular study (a definition of the characteristics of serious viewers of television

---

[7] José M. de Vera, "Serious Television Drama: The Japanese Audience, Its Composition and Characteristics," *Monumenta Nipponica*, Tokyo: Sophia University, Vol. XXIII, Numbers 1–2, pp. 90–101.

Chapter Six. Television Generation

drama) the population was divided into four groups: heavy viewers of drama, light viewers of drama, viewers of entertainment chiefly, and viewers of serious programs. The heavy viewers of drama (and indiscriminate viewers) were at one extreme of the spectrum with 4 hours and 18 minutes of daily watching; the group of light viewers of drama with 2 hours and 30 minutes were at the other extreme. In between came the entertainment-oriented group averaging 3 hours and 48 minutes a day and the serious-minded group with 2 hours and 54 minutes. A multitude of surveys has tried to determine the number of Japanese who watch TV every day, and the numbers seem to be of these magnitudes:

WEEKDAYS:	Morning	41,000,000
	Afternoon	32,000,000
	Evening	61,000,000
SUNDAYS:	Morning	37,000,000
	Afternoon	45,000,000
	Evening	63,000,000

The reasons why the morning audiences are slightly smaller on Sundays and holidays (37,000,000) than on weekdays (41,000,000) are only too obvious. In past years, the afternoon and evening audiences of TV were larger on Sundays than on weekdays. This trend, however, has been reversed in recent years, reflecting a greater affluence among the Japanese and more diversity in leisure patterns. Three hours on weekdays is the TV time for 25.1% of the population while on Sundays only 20.9% spend that much time on TV. The two-hours group on weekdays is composed of 31.6% of the population, but on Sundays it goes down to 17.8%. (Exhibits 3 and 4.) A steady increase has taken place over the years (Exhibit 5), and the phenomenon is general. (Exhibit 6.)

EXHIBIT 3

TIME SPENT WATCHING TV

WEEKDAYS (NOV. 1971)

(Sample: 2587, between 13 and 69 years of age)

	ALL	MALE						FEMALE					(%)
		13-19	20-29	30-39	40-49	50-59	60-69	13-19	20-29	30-39	40-49	50-59	60-69
1 hour	20.0	18.9	30.2	21.1	20.5	18.4	18.3	24.0	13.9	18.2	21.6	17.9	16.4
2 hours	31.6	36.2	32.4	33.1	35.9	29.7	26.9	33.5	32.8	31.5	32.8	23.5	22.9
3 hours	21.1	29.6	21.3	25.8	26.5	33.5	24.0	27.5	26.1	21.8	24.7	20.7	20.7
4 hours	11.2	9.2	7.6	13.8	9.4	7.6	14.4	8.5	14.3	10.3	10.4	15.1	15.0
5 hours	5.4	2.6	4.0	1.5	2.6	5.7	5.8	4.0	5.6	7.6	5.0	12.8	11.4
6 hours	1.8	0.5	1.8	0.4	0.0	1.3	3.8	0.5	2.1	3.3	1.2	3.9	4.3
7 hours	1.0	0.5	0.9	0.0	0.4	0.0	1.0	0.0	1.4	1.8	0.8	3.9	0.7
8 hours	0.4	0.5	0.0	0.4	0.0	1.3	0.0	0.0	0.7	0.6	0.4	0.0	0.7
9 hours	0.7	0.5	0.0	1.1	0.4	0.0	1.9	0.0	0.0	1.2	0.8	0.6	2.1
Don't watch	2.1	1.5	1.8	1.8	2.1	1.3	2.9	1.5	3.1	2.1	1.9	1.1	4.3
Don't know	0.8	0.0	0.0	1.1	2.1	1.3	1.0	0.5	0.0	1.5	0.4	0.6	1.4

Source: Same as Exhibit 2.

EXHIBIT 4

TIME SPENT WATCHING TV

SUNDAYS AND HOLIDAYS (NOV. 1971)

(Sample: 2587, between 13 and 69 years of age)

| | ALL | MALE | | | | | | FEMALE | | | | | (%) |
		13-19	20-29	30-39	40-49	50-59	60-69	13-19	20-29	30-39	40-49	50-59	60-69
1 hour	8.7	4.1	10.2	5.1	9.4	6.3	10.6	4.0	7.7	13.3	12.4	10.1	9.3
2 hours	17.8	16.8	20.0	17.1	15.8	12.0	18.3	9.5	20.6	18.2	24.7	14.0	23.6
3 hours	20.9	16.3	22.2	21.8	21.8	25.3	16.3	26.0	21.6	22.7	20.5	17.9	12.1
4 hours	15.7	22.4	18.2	16.0	17.1	16.5	10.6	16.5	16.4	12.4	12.7	16.2	12.1
5 hours	14.0	17.9	13.3	12.7	15.0	14.6	11.5	22.5	12.9	11.5	10.4	16.2	12.1
6 hours	7.2	7.7	8.0	10.2	6.0	5.7	5.8	8.5	8.0	5.2	5.4	8.9	7.1
7 hours	2.5	4.1	0.9	2.2	0.9	5.1	3.8	3.0	3.1	2.1	1.9	2.8	2.1
8 hours	2.1	3.1	1.8	2.2	2.6	1.9	1.9	3.5	1.0	2.4	2.3	0.6	2.1
9 hours	4.1	4.1	2.2	5.5	3.4	5.1	9.6	3.0	3.5	4.2	2.3	4.5	5.7
Don't watch	2.1	1.5	1.8	1.1	1.7	2.5	1.0	2.5	4.2	1.8	1.9	1.7	2.9
No holiday	2.9	0.5	0.9	4.0	3.4	3.2	5.8	0.0	0.7	2.7	3.5	3.9	10.0
Don't know	2.0	1.5	0.4	2.2	3.0	1.9	4.8	1.0	0.3	3.3	1.9	3.4	0.7

Source: Same as Exhibit 2.

EXHIBIT 5
YEARLY CHANGE OF TELEVISION EXPOSURE RATIOS
(average from Monday to Friday; between 10 and 69 years of age)
(1963–1972)

	FORENOON	AFTERNOON	EVENING	DAILY
June 1963	48%	38%	86%	–%
June 1964	51	39	82	–
July 1965	57	45	84	91
June 1966	61	44	84	92
June 1967	63	44	84	94
June 1968	62	47	83	92
June 1969	63	43	82	92
June 1970	64	40	81	91
June 1971	67.3	47.6	87.9	95.4
June 1972	67.0	47.3	86.4	94.3

Sources: 1963–1967: "Televiewing by Japanese People," *Studies in Broadcasting*, Tokyo: 1969, p. 60.
After 1967: *Annual Survey*, Tokyo: NHK Public Opinion Culture Institute, various years.

EXHIBIT 6
TELEVISION EXPOSURE RATIOS
(for different demographic attributes, between 10 and 69 years of age)
(JUNE 1971)

	FORENOON	AFTERNOON	EVENING	DAILY
Farmers	68%	66%	89%	96%
Private business owners	63	61	87	95
Large-size enterprise workers				
Blue-collar	73	33	87	96
White-collar	69	24	83	93
Small and medium-size enterprise workers				
Blue-collar	68	44	90	96
White-collar	65	30	87	96
Housewives	77	75	90	96
Elementary school children	63	43	91	97
Junior high school students	63	26	88	95
Senior high school students	52	19	85	90
Unemployed	72	70	89	96

Source: *Annual Survey*, Tokyo: NHK Public Opinion Culture Institute, 1971, p. 3.

Chapter Six. Television Generation

The most popular program on NHK could have an audience of 32,000,000, as is the case of "*Taikōki*". A popular comedy program like "*Owarai San-nin Gumi*" attracts 24,000,000 viewers, and Sunday's "*Uta no Grand Show*" 30,000,000. In 1971 the audience for the news at 7 p.m. was 26,187,000, and the drama "*Haru no Sakamichi*", broadcast on Sunday at 8:00 p.m., had 19,227,000 viewers.[8] Naturally, not all the programs have such large audiences. To take some examples from NHK programs, "Sunday University" and "Let's Speak Correct Japanese" have no measurable audiences because they do not individually reach a minimum of 73,000 viewers. Channel 3's "Religious Hour" on Sundays at 7 a.m. has an estimated audience of around 73,000.[9]

As far as the viewing habits of children go, a survey of 1961 shows that by the age of two, one out of ten children was making fairly regular use of TV. By the age of three, four out of ten children were regular viewers. By the time children reached school age, almost all were acquainted with TV. In comparing this survey with a similar one made in the United States, we find that the Japanese children begin regular use of TV one year earlier than their American counterparts. Data gathered by the Ministry of Education show that 11% of Tokyo children were making use of TV by the age of one. At the age of three, 71% of the Tokyo children were TV viewers compared to 37% of the San Francisco children. At the age of five, 98% of the Tokyo children, compared to 82% of the San Francisco children, were using TV.[10] The average time of TV viewing for children is three hours a day, or a total of 1,095 hours a year—just five hours less than the 1,100 hours required by the Ministry of Education for a school year.[11]

---

[8] *TV, Radio Bangumi Shichōritsu Chōsa* ('Survey of Audience-rating for TV and Radio Programs'), Tokyo: NHK Hōsō Yoron Chōsajo, June 1971.

[9] *TV and Radio Audience Rating, July 1965*, Tokyo: The Nippon Hōsō Kyōkai, p.48.

[10] Takeo Furu, "Research on Television and the Child in Japan," *Studies of Broadcasting 1964*, Tokyo: The Nippon Hōsō Kyōkai, p. 104.

[11] Mitoji Nishimoto, *TV Kyōiku Tenbō* ('A View of Educational TV'), Tokyo: Nippon Hōsō Kyōiku, 1963, pp. 22–23.

While it is difficult to assess what people *de facto* learn from their daily TV diet, their opinions on the impact of TV on people's lives are not too hard to obtain. Confining figures for the moment to TV drama, more than 66% of men and 70% of women in Tokyo believe that people do learn from watching TV.[12] Only 17% among men and 13% among women said that people learn nothing from TV. When confronted, however, with the question of whether they learn anything from TV drama, 42% of the men and 46% of the women answered positively, whereas 58% and 53%, respectively, denied any learning. Interestingly enough, most respondents admit that "the others" learn from TV drama but deny that they themselves learn anything. An analysis of the answers leads toward the following conclusions: in answer to the question of whether other people learn from watching TV drama, the respondents projected their own experience. But when asked about themselves, most respondents demurred, probably feeling that to confess learning from TV was an admission of weakness and superficiality. To learn from books or from professional teachers is something socially acceptable, and few individuals are ashamed to confess that they are still learning, no matter how old or famous. But TV is different. It has been called the idiot-box, and recognition of its educational potentiality belongs to an inner circle of experts. For the man in the street to admit learning from TV—especially from TV drama— is to damage his self-image. The negative answer is an unconscious self-protection. If these reflections are true, the percentage who unconsciously feel that they learn from serious TV drama is given in answer to the question regarding "the others".

When asked what "other people" learn from TV, men believe that under the influence of TV people come to understand the social trends of our age (44%), learn "new human relations" (43%), "concrete ways of overcoming difficulties in life" (33%), and open their eyes to the shortcomings of a feudalistic tradition and back-

---

[12] José M. de Vera, *op. cit.*

ward customs of the past (32%). Women list "new human relations" (45%), "human love" (38%), "realization of the shortcomings of a feudalistic tradition and backward customs of the past" (35%), "new humanism" (35%), and "concrete ways of overcoming difficulties in life and getting over feelings of unhappiness" (35%), as the main lessons derived from watching TV drama.

People seem to learn from TV specific techniques more often than values. Of 375 answers, 231 gave examples from the realm of practical knowledge (61.6%) as against 144 (38.4%) who claim to have received insights of a deeper nature from TV.

In the first group (specific knowledge) a favorite subject with women was the progress they made in cooking thanks to the TV programs. Child rearing, health care, awareness of some legal problems involved in everyday life, useful suggestions on how to spend or administer income, recent trends in social etiquette, improvement of vocabulary, ways of carrying through a conversation, and hair styles were the topics most often mentioned by the women of the first group.

Men referred frequently to the usefulness of watching TV programs dealing with driving and traffic problems, analysis of business conditions and fluctuations of prices, lessons on how to play musical instruments or improve golf techniques, expansion of vocabulary mainly in the fields of new things and new discoveries.

In the second group (getting deeper insights from TV programs) there is no striking difference between males and females although men are more explicit than women. It is common to find expressions like these: "While watching the home-drama, I ask myself how it applies to my own life." "Looking at the bright atmosphere of some drama I resolved to make my own family atmosphere more pleasant and warm." As a consequence of this frame of mind in watching TV, many viewers claim to have acquired a better understanding of human relations and to have improved their own relations with friends and relatives. "I changed my way of behaving toward my mother." "It helped me to understand my youngsters."

A second pattern of answers among respondents is connected with a better understanding of themselves. "Watching the characters of some drama, I came to understand myself." "I discovered new insights into my own life." "I found solutions to personal problems watching TV." "I was inspired by a TV drama to live in a fuller way." "You get a new way of looking at things: a wider horizon in your life." Men attributed to TV their "increased interest in public affairs, international relations and politics."

The degree of satisfaction with the present diet of TV is overwhelming. Favorable reactions in Tokyo ("very satisfied", "satisfied") outnumbered unfavorable ones almost 4 to 1, although the noncommittal group was the largest one. This feeling of satisfaction seems to remain unperturbed even when commercials pile up in the middle of a program.

How people react to commercials

A SAMPLE of housewives in Tokyo and Kanazawa city answered several questions regarding commercials on TV.[13] A very high percentage of them (98%) said that in their families there was somebody who liked the commercials, while the presence of a member of the family who had strong dislike for them was true only in less than half (46%). The liking of commercials is clearly related to the age of viewers. Up to 14 years of age the number of children who dislike commercials is negligible, but beyond that point the curve begins to rise rapidly to reach its climax at the 40–49 bracket. Only 3% of the husbands in the Tokyo sample liked the commercials, against 28% who disliked them strongly. The wives showed less negative feelings towards the commercials (8% disliked them strongly) and more interest in them (4%).

Something similar can be said about "imitating" the TV ads. A

[13] *Shufu to CM* ('Housewives and Commercials'), Tokyo: Nihon Minkan Hōsō Renmei, May 1968, pp. 24–25.

surprising percentage (94%) said that somebody in the family imitates the commercials, but we find that the impersonators are children, mainly between 3 and 5 years of age.

Are TV ads a matter of conversation in the home? A small group (2%) makes them a frequent matter of conversation, while a somewhat larger group (8%) never takes them up. Those who occasionally talk about commercials are almost evenly divided with those who rarely talk about them (40% and 48% respectively).

It is not too hard to pronounce a sentence in favor of or against a TV ad; but when pressed for some specific reasons to justify their judgement, people are quite often at a loss. With the help of a list of possible reasons, the respondents of the Tokyo sample gave the following answers in regard to their liking of concrete commercials:[14]

1) The rhythm; music
2) The actor
3) The scenery
4) The wording
5) Good feeling
6) Sense of intimacy
7) Clear explanation of the product
8) Interesting
9) Soft sell
10) Refreshing

The reasons for disliking concrete TV ads were as follows:

1) The story
2) Hard sell
3) The wording
4) Bad for children
5) The actor
6) Unpleasant feeling
7) Stupid
8) Aggressive

Mothers are not infallible in interpreting the likings or dislikings of their children, but certainly they are keen observers of their behavior. As interpreted by a sample of Tokyo mothers, the reasons why their children watch TV ads are as follows, in order of importance:

1) Rhythmical ads
2) Ads with actors or actresses the children like

[14] *Ibid.*, p. 14.

3) Comic ads
4) Ads in programs they normally watch
5) Ads popular among their friends and classmates
6) Ads about articles of interest for children
7) Ads with action
8) Ads which are talked about in the house
9) Ads which appear again and again[15]

This classification does not avoid some overlapping as the music of some commercials, for instance, can be popular among classmates—item number 5—and in this way come to the attention of a particular child. The same can be said regarding items number 2 and number 3 because quite often the actors whom children like are comedians.

It is not clear whether the same reasons are valid for adults' commercial viewing, but their expectations towards advertising emphasize the information and the utility of the product rather than the entertaining aspect of the commercials. (Exhibit 7.)

EXHIBIT 7
EXPECTATIONS REGARDING ADVERTISING
(1968)

	ELECTRICAL APPLIANCES	PHARMA- CEUTICALS	COSMETICS	COOKIES & SWEETS	CLOTHING
Amusing and entertaining	1%	2%	9%	46%	7%
Precise and right explanation	59	73	62	21	51
Useful knowledge	29	16	9	6	30
Without too much exaggeration	7	2	7	6	4
Modest rather than glamorous	4	10	14	21	8

Source: *Shufu to CM* ('Housewives and Commercials'), Tokyo: Nihon Minkan Hōsō Renmei, May 1968, p. 25.

[15] *Ibid.*, p. 23.

Chapter Six. Television Generation

The proof of the pudding is in the eating, and the justification of the high expenses involved in advertising is, in the eyes of the sponsors, the effectiveness in selling the product. A number of housewives were asked whether they had bought some product motivated by TV commercials. The 1,010 cases recorded have been divided in Exhibit 8.

EXHIBIT 8

PURCHASING MOTIVATED BY TV COMMERCIALS
(1968)

PRODUCT	CASES	%
Total	1,010	100.0
Food	593	58.7
Pharmaceuticals	102	10.1
Domestic utensils	61	6.1
Cosmetics	42	4.2
Clothing	3	4.2
Others	209	20.7

Source: *Ibid.*, p. 29.

Even if a housewife buys a product, it is not always on her own initiative. Among the 1,010 cases studied, children were responsible for 634 items, husbands for 94, and wives for the remaining 270.

In a survey conducted during the summer of 1968 in Kitakyushu, a group of researchers developed the concept of "market leader" to signify the type of housewife who takes the initiative in buying and influences the purchasing behavior of the people around her, who are called "followers". The findings of this survey are very similar to the classical results of the "opinion leader" studies in the United States.[16] The "market-leader" is more exposed to TV than the "followers" (4 hours a day against 2 hours 50 minutes), but is also more inclined to news reporting, educational and cultural programs, baseball games, and western movies. There is no difference between

[16] Joseph Klapper, *The Effectiveness of Mass Media*, Illinois, U. S. A.: The Free Press of Glencoe, 1960, pp. 32–93.

the housewives classified as "market leaders" and "followers", at least with respect to their liking of home-drama. (Exhibit 9.)

EXHIBIT 9

FAVORITE PROGRAMS OF LEADERS AND FOLLOWERS
(SUMMER 1968)

	LEADER-TYPE	FOLLOWER-TYPE
News reporting	75.4%	61.7%
Educational Programs	39.1	23.7
Social and cultural programs	56.5	30.0
Home drama	59.4	60.3
Love drama	11.6	18.9
Historical drama	21.7	18.2
Thriller, action drama	36.2	29.8
Comedies	27.5	30.0
Cowboy drama	29.0	19.4
Serious drama	24.6	25.9
Popular songs	20.3	21.3
Popular music	23.2	21.1
Musical variety	14.5	9.7
Local songs, *Noh* music	10.1	14.3
Classical music	23.2	17.9
Quiz game	37.7	34.9
Cartoon, *contes*	10.1	9.4
Farce, repartee	33.3	34.9
Sumō	13.0	9.2
Boxing, professional wrestling	10.0	7.3
Professional baseball	27.5	16.5
Other sports	17.4	9.4
Total	429	2,163
Sample number	69	413
Choice per capita	6.22	5.24

Source: Minpō Gosha Kenkyūkai, *Nihon no Shichōsha* ('The Japanese Audience'), Part II, Tokyo: Seibundō-Shinkōsha, 1969, p 195.

Chapter Six. Television Generation

The attitude of Japanese "market leaders" regarding TV commercials is definitely more tolerant, interested, and positive than that of other persons, as the following table shows:

	TOTAL	TOLERANT	NEUTRAL	NOT TOLERANT
Leader-type	69	49.3%	46.4%	4.3%
Follower-type	413	32.4%	60.8 %	6.8%

Whether the "market leaders" will become "opinion leaders" in the realm of politics remains to be seen. The indirect influence of TV has been felt in the elections even if the candidates were not allowed to use the medium during their political campaigns. In 1969 the legal restrictions were removed so that TV might become an important tool in the political market. To what extent it will ultimately affect the fabric of Japan's politics is anybody's guess at this stage, although everything points to lasting influence.

TV has certainly entered Japanese life, permeated it, and changed it profoundly. Some visible and measurable indexes of this permeation are clear, but one feels that the real effects lie beyond measurability. As somebody has pointed out, this generation of Japanese who have rejected most of the values considered sacred by their parents a few years ago, is the first generation born under the hegemony of TV. The images, expectations, and sensibility they bring along are not in our maps. The electronic explosion is comparable to the atomic explosion which a quarter of a century ago changed the course of Japanese history.

Creativity in Advertising

TOMOKIYO YAMADA

Where to get your advertising created—Japanese copy: how to get control over the Japanese copy; testing the copy; the name is the game; technique of Japanese copywriting; Kana, Kanji, English mix; the Japanese approach to copy —Advertising art: how to orient yourself to a layout; how to make sense out of Japanese typography; how photography buying is different; illustration, cartoons, design; how to select models; how art work is done; newspapers, magazines, and other printing—Producing television commercials—To pick up or not to pick up

How are you to get the outstanding and creative advertising in Japan that you need? The answer: the same way you get it in the West. You must have

. . . insight into your market and product

. . . superior marketing strategies

. . . realistic advertising objectives

. . . effective implementation by talented staff in
your advertising agency.

As a foreign advertiser in Japan you must add another dimension. You need

. . . deep understanding of the *differences* in the Japanese
advertising craft, language, and cultural attitudes
from the western patterns with which you are familiar.

This additional knowledge and understanding will have to be obtained by you piecemeal, and with great effort. The present chapter will give you a few facts and opinions that you may find useful.

One thing is eminently clear at the outset. Advertising is different in Japan. And understanding its differences is necessary for effective advertising.

Where to get your advertising created

In Japan you have a wide and exotic choice. You can chop up your advertising assignment on a media basis and appoint agencies specializing in a single medium: one agency for magazines, one agency for television, and so on. You will end up with several mini-campaigns and a problem of integration.

You may be persuaded that creative services and media can be divorced. You can get your creative material from a creative shop and then turn it over to a brokerage agency for placement. But you must be prepared to pay a double fee.

Or you can go to one of the western-style "marketing" agencies that give you the same kind of advertising service that you are used to. They service only one client in the product field, but they go deeper into marketing advice than in the West, because in Japan you need depth.

Successful and creative advertising is produced in Japan using any one or a combination of these means. Generally speaking, the western marketer has gravitated sooner or later to the full-service shops.

You have appointed your agency, and now you get to work. Surprisingly, you will be talking the same trade language, for the most part. The Japanese advertising profession has borrowed extensively from the West. Japanese trade terms consist of four types:

Chapter Seven. Creativity in Advertising

1) *Western terms.* Over half of the terms are of this type, for example: headline, readership, survey, copywriter, illustration, etc.

2) *Japanese terms.* Pure Japanese words like *Kōkoku dairiten* (advertising agency), *Baitai* (media), *Shōhisha* (consumer), etc.

3) *Compound Japanese and English terms.* Such as *Mākettingu senryaku* (marketing strategy), *Shōhin tesuto* (product test), etc.

4) *English contractions and combinations.* These are essentially new words made by the Japanese tendency to shorten western words: *Gyara* (guarantee or fee), *Kineko* (kinescope recording), *Masukomi* (mass communication), *Rokehan* (location hunting), etc.

Though the same western terms are used, you must not assume that they always have the same meaning as in the West. For example, the western AD is close to the Japanese "designer". The "copywriter" works mostly on print advertising. When he works on broadcasts he is referred to as "CM writer". The western marketer is advised to take the terms as they come.

Japanese copy

How will you judge the quality of Japanese copywriting? Unless you are also a Japanese language scholar, you can't. It will take you years to learn the language well enough to appreciate the nuances that separate the mediocre from the great. You will probably be looking at a translation.

Reading a translation takes extraordinary skill. You must make the necessary mental preparation. Understand that what you are reading is a translation, not advertising copy. A *translation* merely changes thoughts from one language to another. *Advertising copy* is skillful writing that creatively and persuasively communicates concepts to particular consumers in their own language and idiom.

The translation you will be reading was probably done by a Japanese native who is an English language scholar. He learned English by the book and not from actual experience. The translation will be grammatically correct and reasonably readable, but it will reflect the scholar with a tendency toward "bookishness". It is certainly not copy.

Occasionally you will spot word combinations that do not exist in English. This is not necessarily due to the lack of skill of the translator. Many words and concepts are not transferable. Such odd word combinations as "rich comfort" and "outing wear" are the closest renderings in English of clear Japanese concepts that don't exist in English. You will know them after a while because they occur frequently. In addition, there are certain linguistic differences that make translation difficult, such as reverse word order and the constant omission of subjects, verbs, and even objects. While it is sufficient in Japanese to say "Please on your table" *(shoku-taku ni dōzo)*, translation into English requires the insertion of an extra word for comprehension: "Please serve (mustard) on your table."

In reading a translation you should go after the *content* and not the style. Look for the basic selling points or appeals. They should all be there. In addition, a certain logical sequence in the presentation of the message should be evident. These are points you can comment on profitably from the translation. When you have an experienced and competent professional Japanese copywriter from an agency, you have to assume that the copy is correct in style and has excitement in the Japanese original.

You are in trouble if you insist on personally rewriting *(in English)* the translation copy to demonstrate the "feel" that you want. By the time it was turned back into Japanese through the language filter it would be worse than the original, for your own ideas are based on a different means of persuasion. So despite your good intentions you may be doing yourself a disservice.

Chapter Seven. Creativity in Advertising

EVEN though you can't read the original Japanese copy and must rely on translation, there are techniques you can use to exercise control over the copy. Insist on a document in English stating the copy objectives, the main selling promise, and the copy points in the order of importance. These are concepts and can be readily translated. In fact, you can share in their development.

After you approve these, give the Japanese copywriter the freedom of implementation. Insist that the basic points be communicated, but don't pick on the fine points of expression.

You will probably have a Japanese member of your staff approving the Japanese copy from the agency. This person should be selected with exceptional care and should receive your complete trust and confidence. But he shouldn't be a writer, or else there is danger of a writing contest.

If instinct tells you that there is something wrong with the copy, what is your recourse? Ask that the copy be tested. If the copy plays back the main selling promises from the consumer, you will have no grounds for complaint.

TESTING THE COPY

YOU are advertising to a consumer that you don't understand. Your agency gives you a campaign and copy that defy western logic. But the decision and final responsibility are yours. That's why foreign marketers rely heavily on testing and are responsible for much of the pioneering and development of advertising research in Japan. Most of the western testing techniques are available and heavily used.

Testing is especially important when you are thinking of using an international theme. Some themes can be used; others can't. When SEVEN-UP's recent slogan "Wet and Wild" was tested, it was found to be unsuitable for Japan. The English term "wet" has a special Japanese meaning: it's used to describe an emotional personality and is always associated with its opposite "dry", which means a clear-cut, frank personality. Similarly, the term "wild" had no meaning to most of the respondents. So the English phrase "Wet and Wild" was hardly the right one to use in Japan to describe the refreshing liveliness of SEVEN-UP. The English term "Fresh and Sharp" was developed, and when this was tested on Japanese it had all the qualities of "Wet and Wild" in western terms.

THE NAME IS THE GAME

ONE of the most important decisions that a foreign marketer will have to make, if the power of decision is his, concerns the name of his product. Naming in Japan is more difficult than in the West because of the extra dimension of the Japanese-English language mix.

Some western names may be unsuited for the Japanese market because of their unpleasant sound or connotation. However, many English names seem to transfer well. The easier to read and pronounce, the better the name. English names are always pronounced in the Japanese style in the market place. PARKER is pronounced *pah-kah* and SCOTTIES becomes *sko-tei*. The western marketer will have to decide exactly how his name should be pronounced in Japanese. He will usually have several alternatives. For example, when Pan American World Airways shortened its name in its advertising to PAN AM it had several choices: "Pa-n-ame", "Pa-n-na-me", "Pa-na-mu", Pa-n-a-mu", and "Pa-n-na-mu". The last was selected.

If new names are to be created for Japan it is better left up to the Japanese, even for western or western-type names. For example, what westerner could come up with names like CALPIS and CREAP for food products? Yet both are market successes in Japan.

TECHNIQUE OF JAPANESE COPYWRITING

JAPANESE copywriting is a difficult craft. The copywriter must communicate in one of the world's most complex and tricky languages. It is actually many languages in one. There are literary and conversational styles. There are male and female styles. There are young and old styles. Add to this the various levels of politeness required and a tremendous influx of English words, and you face notable linguistic complexity.

The chart following shows some of the variations that the English concept "Let's go" can assume in Japanese. These are all part of any copywriter's vocabulary; he must know which form to use to reach a particular target of consumers.

"LET'S GO"

	POLITENESS LEVEL	SEX	AGE & CLASS
Ukagaimashō	Very polite	Both	Adult
Ukagaimashōne	" "	Female	"
Ittemairimashō	Polite	Both	"
Ittemairimashōne	"	Female	"
Mairimashō	"	Both	"
Mairimashōyo	"	Female	"
Ikimashō	Standard	Both	All
Ikimashōne	"	Female	"
Ikimasenka	Friendly polite	Both	"
Ikōyo	Friendly	"	Youth, children
Ikanai?	"	Male	All
Let's go	"	Both	Youth
Ikōze	Rough	Male	Youth

KANA, KANJI, ENGLISH MIX

WRITTEN Japanese consists of three forms: *hiragana, katakana,* and *kanji.* English words must be considered as the fourth form, especially in advertising copy. The first two, *hiragana* and *katakana,* both called *kana,* are Japanese equivalents of the phonetic alphabet. They consist of 46 syllables plus 25 sound variants called sonants and half sonants. All Japanese words, without exception, end in a vowel or the "n" sound. In Japan interesting things happen to English words. The nearest-sounding syllables are used. Thus "hotel" becomes *hoteru* and "grape" becomes *gurēpu.* And unless they're pronounced this way, they are incomprehensible to the Japanese.

Kanji are ideographic forms borrowed from China. Postwar reforms have reduced the number for everyday use to 1,850, but it is still a formidable task to learn them all. Educated Japanese must know many more for normal reading and several readings for each character.

Advertising copy consists of a mix of these three forms, plus a liberal sprinkling of English words.

Hiragana is the form taught earliest in school. It is used for most parts of speech, plus animal and plant names. It has a soft cursive look and an intimate feeling.

Katakana is used for names of foreign words, places, people, and for Japanese words given special emphasis. It is angular in appearance and brittle in feeling.

Kanji or Chinese characters are used for nouns and most parts of speech except for interjections, postpositions, and the like.

English words are used for technical terms, chic phrases, and new ideas that are not expressible in Japanese.

In copywriting the proper mixture and seasoning of these four ingredients are important. *Kanji* is harder to read than *hiragana*; consequently when there are too many *kanji*, the writing is stiff. This danger is especially important in headlines where *kanji* is often replaced by *kana* to give a softer, warmer feeling. Too many *kana* are monotonous and therefore avoided. *Katakana* gives a modern foreign image, but its over-use hampers readability.

A liberal use of English is thought to add chic, and this is especially common in cosmetic advertising. However, such use should not be judged as English copy, for the Japanese meaning could be quite different from the Western meaning. For example, a maker of nail enamels used the product banner "Tender Passion". In Japan "passion" connotes none of the sexual overtones usually associated with it in the West. It has more of the meaning of "ardor", which combined with "tender" makes a delicate appeal to Japanese women.

In Japanese package copy, English is used extensively. In fact, some Japanese packages do not have any Japanese copy at all. Historically many consumer goods such as cigarettes, soaps, and cosmetics were first imported from the West. Even after the Japanese started making the same products, they didn't sell well unless they were packaged in a western style. After the war, because of the influence of the Occupation and the institution of compulsory English-language education in the public schools, this trend has continued, especially among youthful, western beauty products. As a consequence, many western marketers, though their products are made entirely in Japan, choose to use the same English labels and packaging as they use in the West.

Nevertheless, all the English copy on the packages or in the advertising is not meant for reading. Sometimes it is merely used for decorative purposes.

THE JAPANESE APPROACH TO COPY

GENERALLY speaking, Japanese copy is more polite in tone than the English. Any copy automatically sets up a social relationship between author and reader. The copy produced by the banks and insurance companies is especially polite.

A conversational style is found in many types of advertisement, especially those directed towards teen-agers. Copy directed to young unmarried women is soft and romantic. Headlines are written in a conversational or literary style. Some conversational feeling is found in the text. Copy to married women is usually written in a soft, warm style. For some package goods, however, strong language can be used in headlines because Japanese housewives, like housewives anywhere else in the world, are realistically concerned with economy. For the young man, copy should be dynamic. For mature men, it should be polite. All in all, there is much more care in writing to a specific target in Japan than in the West.

Japanese expressions are often illogical, abstract, and oblique. The direct approach and hard sell are not liked. Imperative phrases such as "Go U.S.A." or "Drink Cola" are rude and never used. They are softened to "Let's go to U.S.A." or "Let's drink Cola".

The Japanese dislike direct comparison with their competition, even though this reserve is being steadily chipped away, especially by foreign marketers. More and more competitive copy is being written in Japan. For example, the word *dake*, meaning "only", is beginning to be used frequently when claiming an exclusive feature. It's a bit jarring to the Japanese ear, but it's probably the sound of the future.

Still, side by side comparison with a competitor's product, direct or implied, is forbidden by the Fair Trade Commission code. Comparisons must be made only between one's own products, such as a new model against a previous model.

There are many Japanese regulatory agencies restraining excesses in copy. Any copy on drug products must be checked by the Medical Department of the Ministry of Health and Welfare. Any contest or prize promotion must abide by rules set up by the Fair Trade Commission. Banking, photographic, electric, automotive, and other industries have self-regulatory standards on copy. Major media have copy standards which are enforced religiously and broadly. For example, PAN AM could not run this headline in a leading newspaper:

> "Three airlines fly to Hawaii—
> One of them is the World's
> Most experienced Airline."

It was considered too competitive. The following suffers a bit in translation, but it is the headline that ran.

> "On the Hawaiian air route—
> One company is the World's
> Most Experienced Airline."

No Japanese copywriter sits down before a typewriter to bang out copy. A Japanese typewriter exists, but it's a noisy machine with

5,425 faces, and it is hardly conducive to the generation of ideas. The Japanese copywriter sits down before copy sheets and uses a method quite efficient. It is based on the fact that in Japanese typography each character, no matter how complex, takes one unit of space. There is no attempt made for proportional spacing as in the West. So it is possible to write accurately for a given space. Except for headlines the sentences and words can be broken anywhere.

The copywriter uses copy sheets calculated for 200 or 400 spaces. There is general agreement as to what copy lengths are right for the space and for easy communication. For example, a spread page would normally require one 200-space copy sheet. Phrases should usually be shorter than two lines of copy sheet.

Advertising art

How will you judge the quality of Japanese advertising art? You will have an easier time with art than with the copy because the visual language and procedure of Japan, though different, are easier to comprehend. Practically any form of art or photographic technique is available. The Japanese artist is imaginative and technically proficient. The quality of Japanese printing is excellent. The color reproduction in the average magazine and newspaper is better than the average in the West.

HOW TO ORIENT YOURSELF TO A LAYOUT

READING the layout is the same as in the West, except for one difference. You have to orient yourself to a vertical or horizontal setting. If the layout is set vertically, the eye should start from the upper right and read down and left. The headline should be on the right, and the logo generally on the bottom left.

When the type is set horizontally, the same visual flow applies as in the western layout. The logo is normally on the lower right. Though vertical and horizontal settings are often mixed in the same layout, it is advisable to make one dominate.

Since in most Japanese magazines the back is the front, the approach to the ad as the pages are flipped is from the right. When the magazine is set up like western magazines, the approach is from the left.

HOW TO MAKE SENSE OUT OF JAPANESE TYPOGRAPHY

TYPOGRAPHY may be the strangest element to you. Most, if not all of it, will be unintelligible. A few English words will stick out disproportionately to their assumed effect on the Japanese. After examination, you will notice that the type falls into normal western categories of headline, subhead, copy and signature. The fundamental difference is that in Japan copy can be set horizontally or vertically, or both.

The wide variety of type faces available in the West are not available to the Japanese typographer simply because of the extremely large number of characters required for a single Japanese font—over 2,000! However, there are several basic families available. The *Minchō* is roughly comparable to the Roman family of types in the West. It has thick and thin strokes and spurs which can be compared to serifs. The most traditional and Chinese of faces, the *Minchō* is most commonly used for body copy because of its legibility. The other major family available in Japan is the *Gochikku*, which is roughly comparable to western Gothics. Its characters are simplified so that there are no width variations in the strokes. The *Gochikku* is used chiefly in headlines. Generally speaking, it gives a modern feeling to copy whereas *Minchō* gives a traditional, softer feeling.

Hand lettering is also used in Japan as in the West to create a distinctive quality. Occasionally, when a traditional effect is required, calligraphy or brush lettering is used.

Japanese typography does not have the good "color" or even quality enjoyed by fine typography in the West because, as mentioned earlier, Japanese typography is not proportionally spaced. The most simple single stroke *kanji* is given the same space as the most complicated 23-stroke character. This disproportion results in a splotchy look on the copy block.

In Japan English words are used either in western typography or in Japanese *katakana.* Occasionally English type is set vertically, forcing the reader to tip the page sideways in order to read it. When there are many English words, the Japanese text is set horizontally.

Because *kanji* are ideographic, it is possible to read a headline very fast. In fact, copy can be scanned quickly by reading the *kanji* only.

HOW PHOTOGRAPHY BUYING IS DIFFERENT

PHOTOGRAPHY is of a fairly high standard in Japan. There are professional photographers specializing in foods, fashion, and editorial work.

However, there is an important difference. In Japan, a photographer, called a *kameraman,* performs only a small part in the total photographic assignment. The agency selects models, gathers props and costumes, arranges schedules, hires auxiliary help, and sets up shots. The cameraman comes in at the end, arranges the lights, sets up the camera, tinkers a bit with the props, and shoots. The cameraman doesn't charge as much as cameramen in America, but in view of his small contribution he is adequately paid. There are pressures, especially from western-style agencies, to force a greater contribution and responsibility from the cameraman, but he will not change overnight. Meanwhile, you or your agency can count on doing much of the cameraman's work.

Very few cameramen in Japan have their own studios. This is a factor that severely restricts the quality of Japanese photography. Most work must be done in rental studios, which are few and must be scheduled in advance. The average rental time is just enough to set up equipment, take a few shots, tear down, and get out. Usually other photographic groups are waiting their turn to use the same facilities. This factor puts severe psychological pressures on photographic work. It limits shots, discourages elaborate set-ups, and makes reshooting a major project. This system explains why Japanese studio photography is almost always conceptually simple. On location Japanese photography is excellent. On the whole Japan is a photogenic country and Japanese photographers are skillful in making the most of this asset.

The Japan Photographers' Society (JPS) prescribes certain copyright regulations in regard to photography. Editorial copyright belongs to the photographer and, after its use, is returned to him. In advertising, however, the rights are sold outright to the purchaser. But it is advisable to reach a full understanding with the photographer in advance.

ILLUSTRATION, CARTOONS, DESIGN

JAPANESE standards of advertising illustration are good, but there is a tendency to swing with the vogue of the West. Some of the technically most proficient illustrators draw for pulp magazines in black and white. Hand painting of giant building-size movie posters is a lively art, comparable in quality to the painted bulletin school of the United States West Coast.

Given a lively cartoon tradition, in recent years Japan has experienced an explosion of comic magazines targeted to the male audience. Although they use very poor paper stock and virtually no color, the effect of the magazines is dynamic. Their stories and illustrations are full of action and eroticism. Cartoons are becoming prevalent also in television advertising and print advertising. There is a definite cartoon-style in Japan which is difficult to explain, except that Japanese drawings tend to be more linear than those of the West.

Emerging from a long and excellent tradition, Japanese designers are excellent, as Japanese packages and posters testify. In advertising, however, the influence of designers has not always been good. In the early days of advertising, when designers were ad-makers, ads had a strongly graphic appearance. Recently, however, layouts are conceived primarily from the point of view of communication. The legacy of design is still evident in many Japanese ads, but it remains to enhance, rather than to dominate.

HOW TO SELECT MODELS

YOUR conception of a good model will be different from that of the Japanese. Model selection in Japan is a delicate area full of traps.

Japanese advertising is still concerned with an "ideal world", and models are selected because they represent attractive physical types. "Real life" casting is rare except in young and old people. Maybe the Japanese tradition of politeness determines the issue: if TV intrudes into the home, let it be polite and conveyed by nice people. Or if young people cast their own ideals . . . the tall western-looking Japanese must exemplify modern products and a refined clientele must seek Japanese products. "Real life" casting is still an unexplored frontier in Japan.

In advertising fashions or beauty products, the model business is dominated by mixed-bloods, half Japanese and half Caucasian. These models have the attractive features, figures, and movements that the Japanese admire and aspire to. Moreover, they have an indefinable Japanese quality that evokes empathy. Sought after by fashion people because western clothes fit them well, they are desired by cosmetic makers because of their exotic look. All in all, such models are rare.

Now, models call the shots. Shooting schedules are set up around their availability. Popular models are booked solid, and work with them must be scheduled well in advance. In Japan, model selection is best left up to the Japanese.

The Japanese seem to respond more sharply to seasonal changes than westerners do, and Japanese designers exploit this response by being careful about seasonal colors of sky, plants, light, and clothing. For the Japanese there are marked seasonal changes of wardrobe throughout the year. Traditionally, on June 1 all the school girls and boys in Japan change their school uniforms from dark to white; on October 1 they change back to dark.

HOW ART WORK IS DONE

THE Japanese designer does not use the T-square, the most used instrument of his western counterpart. Instead, he uses two triangles in pairs to get his verticals and horizontals. They work out just as well. The omnipresent western photostat is also missing. Japanese photocopies are cheaper and better, though they take a little time. Otherwise, everything else in the Japanese designer's paraphernalia is the same as in the westerner's. Japanese layouts are made to a particular size according to a very rational system based on cuts from paper stock determined by the Japanese Industry Standards. There are two standard sizes, A and B. A–1 signifies half of a full sheet, A–2 half of A–1, A–3 half of A–2, and so on.

The following lists standard sizes in Japan, and their main uses.

A–1 Calendars and posters
A–4 Music sheets
A–5 Books and magazines
A–6 Pocket books

B–2 Calendars and posters
B–3 Car cards
B–4 Graphic magazines
B–5 Weekly magazines
B–6 Books

NEWSPAPERS, MAGAZINES, AND OTHER PRINTING

IN newspaper advertising Japanese columns are horizontal, not vertical as in the West. There are 15 columns altogether. The sizes most generally used are full page, full 10 columns, full 7 columns, full 5 columns, and full single column. Half columns in each of these sizes are also used.

To the western advertiser the significance of this method is that any adaptations from western advertising must be completely redone to fit the Japanese horizontal proportions. It's quite a trick to change a single-column western vertical into a single-column Japanese horizontal. Sometimes it can't be done.

Japanese magazines are not as large as western ones and the reproductions in any may range from poor to excellent. Magazines can use up to three printing processes in the same issue. Color work is by offset or rotogravure, black and white by roto and letterpress.

Color and rotogravure black and white reproductions are excellent. Letterpress reproduction is not too good because the letterpress sections use newsprint quality paper. For these sections the art is treated as if for a newspaper ad.

Deadlines for material done for magazines is 40 days before publication date for the monthlies and a month ahead for the weeklies. Engravings are rarely made from color photographic prints. Color transparencies are used instead. Transparency retouching services are available, but they are not developed to the western degree. The engraver himself makes much of the correction.

Japanese printing quality on P.O.P. (point of purchase) and other materials is excellent. Almost any work done in the West can be produced just as well or better by the Japanese printer.

One important thing to consider in P.O.P. is that, because of the very small size of most stores, P.O.P. has a tendency also to be small in size and vertical in design. As a consequence, the dangler is one of the most popular Japanese forms.

Producing television commercials

MAKING television commercials in Japan is not as costly as in the United States, but it can still take a big chunk out of a production budget. Costs are rocketing. As yet, however, because there are no union, pension, or residual payments, budgeting is somewhat easier.

Estimates from production houses for commercials are almost

like contracts; that is, you can expect the supplier to stay within the budget, barring acts of God like the weather. At any rate, you won't get any money back if the expenses are less than the budget.

Like the still photographers, most of the Japanese production studios are rented. Designers do an adequate job of building sets and the quality of interior camerawork and direction is fair. However, Japanese crews work best out of doors. The crews are energetic and work hard and long, making up for some of the apparent lack of professionalism compared to the buttoned-up, clock-oriented crews of the West.

In Japan 500 to 600 television commercials are made every month of every type and variety. Some of them you may like and understand, and some of them you will never understand.

There seems to be a frantic quality about Japanese television commercials. Every conceivable gimmick is used. A lot of it is due to the jam-up during station breaks where the advertiser must get his message across in 15 seconds, or 5 seconds! However, many fine Japanese commercials are produced that are equal to those anywhere.

The same types of commercials are found as in the West. Such differences as do exist occur more in form than in content. For example, many Japanese commercials are based on universally understood humor, but many others are based on unique Japanese humor, such as the *rakugo* that may be baffling to the westerner. There is less hard sell than in the West, and more use of mood. Indeed, it is often said that the Japanese consumer buys more from his heart than from his head. Since you will doubtless be called into the never ending dialogue implicit here, you are forewarned now that your western reasoning may be held against you as over-simplistic or obviously insensitive. Although they may be sufficient in the West, commercials built on reason alone are not enough in Japan. Just as all purchases and gifts must be nicely wrapped in Japan, all commercial messages must be softened, must be made more acceptable with emotional concomitants.

[162]

Chapter Seven. Creativity in Advertising

The voice of the Japanese female announcer is pitched higher than her counterpart in the West. A Japanese female voice is charming when the speaker is in full sight, but the disembodied off-screen voice can sound like the chatter of chipmunks to the insensitive western ear. Don't worry. It doesn't sound strange to the Japanese, and the speaker is probably communicating your message quite naturally and effectively. Western advertisers normally like lower-pitched female voices for their commercials, but the Japanese reserve such voices for the late late show or for moody cosmetic advertising. For everyday products, the conventional high voices are the best.

For male announcers, the low masculine voices are, as in the West, the best. For children's voices, the more they sound like chipmunks to you the better. The best children's voices are simulated by high-pitched adult females. After a while you will get used to the high voices, and you will start wondering why most female announcers in the West have such unnaturally low husky voices.

To pick up or not to pick up

ONE of the toughest problems that the foreign advertiser must resolve in Japan is whether to pick up home-office advertising material or start from scratch.

There is no easy answer.

It's quite a temptation to want to take a campaign of proven success in other international markets and to say to your agency, "Run it in Japan." You know the contents of the ads because you can read every word. You can save on the artwork because you can re-use the photography taken by some expensive technicians. There is probably a good deal of P.O.P. material that you think can be moderately revised. In addition, it's easy to get home-office approval on the campaign that the home office itself conceived and can understand. It's a complete and beautiful package!

But you may be taking the easy way to disaster.

First of all, success in other markets will not guarantee your success in Japan. Your marketing objectives, competition, and brand image may be, and probably are, different in Japan. You may be marketing physically the same product, but the product image and even its use might be different. The appeals that persuade the westerner may not be the ones that work best with the Japanese.

Your decision should never be made on the basis of economy. It takes just as much time and money, or more, to revise a campaign properly as it does to originate a new one. The photography may use models, settings, or situations that alienate the Japanese. Most likely the phtographs will be copies, not originals, and the reproduction will suffer by comparison with that in the finely printed Japanese magazines. P.O.P. material may be too large for the Japanese stores. You will most certainly have to rescale all the ads to fit Japanese space requirements.

There is danger that your agency might retreat before your enthusiasm, stop thinking, and deliver you "translation" ads. Your world-famous company slogan will sound the same to you when translated back, but in Japanese it may sound odd. The thought is there, but it's not quite Japanese. Neither is the copy. You will never know the difference, but the consumer will.

But this is not to say that advertising can't be imported. It's done every day, and there are many successful examples. But it requires a special kind of handling and skill.

The first requirement is creative people who can fully understand the essence of western advertising and can recreate it with the same vitality in a Japanese context.

The second requirement is that the foreign look and image must enhance your product. A foreign image is often an advantage, and it may be your *only* distinction. Japanese are traditionally very much interested in foreign goods, and ads with a foreign flavor are successful in luxury products such as quality watches, color cosmetics, and fine foods. Foreign ads for modern products directed to the younger audience are also successful.

Chapter Seven. Creativity in Advertising

But for the mass Japanese market of common, medium-priced, everyday packaged goods, it is generally better to stay away from importing the advertising and have it made in Japan, to your specifications.

IN CONCLUSION

THE foreign marketer can advertise successfully in Japan. He should apply his own proved principles of good advertising, but qualify them by an understanding of the *differences* in the Japanese advertising craft, language, and cultural attitudes.

CHAPTER EIGHT

Institutional Promotion
— A Case Study —

YOTARO KOBAYASHI

*Company and market—Marketing plans—Promoting "Xerox":
setting objectives; promotional mix—Advertising: choice
among advertising media; process of advertising activities;
the role of the advertising agency; organization; measuring
effectiveness*

Company and market

FUJI Xerox was first established in 1962 as a 50:50 joint venture company between Fuji Photo Film Co., Ltd., of Japan and Rank Xerox, Ltd., of England. The company is licensed by Rank Xerox to manufacture and market xerographic products in Japan, Korea, Taiwan, Vietnam, Cambodia, Laos, Thailand, Indonesia, and the Philippines. In 1956 Rank Xerox was established on a 50:50 basis between Xerox Corporation of the United States and Rank Organisation of England for the purpose of manufacturing and marketing xerographic products in the eastern hemisphere. The relationship between Xerox and Rank subsequently changed in December 1969 to that of a 51:49 partnership.

After a full ten years of operation the company now grosses over ¥40 billion a year, having grown during those ten years at the compound average annual rate of about 50%. It employs over 6,000 persons in Japan and its other territories of operation. Fuji n, the Japanese parent company, once carried out manufacturing according to a manufacturing agreement, but Fuji Xerox took manufacturing over in 1970 and thus became a full manufacturing/marketing entity.

The market in which Fuji Xerox operates is broadly termed the office copying and duplicating market, which in turn forms part of the office equipment and information industry. Having grown during the past several years at the rate of about 20 to 25% a year, the 1972 market is valued at approximately ¥134 billion and is expected to continue at a similar growth rate in the years to come. A marked trend in the market during recent years has been the phenomenal growth of the electrostatic process of duplication as against the relative stagnation of the once dominant diazo process, although the latter still accounts for more than 30% of the market in value.

Fuji Xerox has been the spearhead in this fast-growing sector of the market, alone accounting for 50% of it, whereas various other electrostatic manufacturers account for the other 50%. The electrostatic sector accounts for about 60% of the whole market, and Fuji Xerox is the single dominant factor in this sector. The electrostatic sector is expected to account for the majority of the market in a couple of years because of the superiority of its process in terms of copy quality and accompanying hardware automaticity.[1]

With the notable exception of Fuji Xerox most Japanese companies market their copiers/duplicators largely through conventional distribution channels, *viz.*, through distributors and retail

---

[1] It should be mentioned that even in the electrostatic sector there are two different processes: one is xerography, commonly called "PPC" for "plain-paper copier", which produces copies on plain bond paper by transferring images from a photoconductive intermediate material; and the other is the RCA method, which employs a special copying paper coated with photoconductive material on which images are directly made. Because of its strong patent position and complex technological expertise involved in the development of xerographic copiers, Xerox had virtual monopoly over the PPC market until late 1970. Today industry experts predict that by the mid-1970s the so-called electrostatic market will practically be a plain-paper copying market.

shops including stationery and department stores. Moreover, they largely sell their products outright to the customers or lease them out through independent leasing companies. Industry tradition has typically been to allocate 60% of total business to supplies (papers, chemicals, etc.) and only 40% to machines, but the advent of relatively more expensive, more profitable electrostatic copiers has changed this pattern considerably by their replacement of obsolescent diazo or other photographic copiers, the total value of which still exceeds that of new supplies. Naturally, as the electrostatic copiers attain a much higher percentage in the overall copier/duplicator distribution, the value ratio of machine-supply will gradually swing back to the conventional level.

The biggest competitor of Fuji Xerox in the Japanese market is Ricoh Co., Ltd. For some years Ricoh has been so big in the industry that its product name, RICOPY, has become a common Japanese verb meaning "to make copies". In fact, the copying/duplicating market in Japan was originally created and developed by Ricoh, and its range of diazo copiers backed up by its aggressive marketing effort truly dominated the market up to a few years ago when excessive price competition in the diazo market put Ricoh in a financial crisis. The company has made a strong comeback, however, on the strength of new electrostatic copiers (RCA type) which it has developed from technologies licensed by American and Australian companies.

Ricoh's annual revenue is roughly ¥75 billion as against Fuji Xerox's ¥42 billion. Nearly 70% of it comes from its range of copiers/duplicators, and the segment is now fast moving from conventional diazo to new electrostatic copiers. Today Ricoh operates 60-odd branches throughout Japan and has about 300 distributors whom it controls financially. Ultimately, at its farthest marketing end it has about 2,000 to 3,000 outlets.[2]

2 The recent upsurge of interest in PPCs has at least temporarily changed the competitive picture in the industry. Ricoh has lagged behind such companies as Konishiroku and Canon in the development of a PPC. It is arguable whether the delay has been*

Unlike its competitors, Fuji Xerox operates only directly through its own sales force of about 500 and a backup service group of about 1,500. These employees operate from the company's 100 branches and depots in Japan. Moreover, the company only rents its products and makes no outright sales. Both of these characteristics, unique in their own right, are the universal marketing policy strictly adhered to by all Xerox companies in the world.

Whether the products are sold or rented and whether they are marketed directly or through distributors, there is a *universal* sales pattern in the industry which is evident in the link that connects customers with the ultimate sales outlets. Simply stated, this is the pattern:

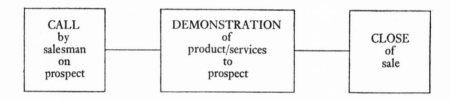

Naturally the salesman must make more than one call before he can bring a prospect to the demonstration stage. And the process can take a couple of days or a couple of months, depending on the salesman's skill, the prospect's needs, or just plain luck. Different from conditions in, say, the electric appliance industry, the volume and weight of sales made through non-personal contacts are extremely small. In the meantime, another process that must be projected against the sales pattern just shown is the pros-

*caused chiefly by technological problems or by marketing problems in the light of the company's need to avoid the self-obsolescence of the RCA-type process in which it invested heavily. In any case, Ricoh may feel consequences of the delay through 1973 and 1974, but is yet likely to come back very strongly as a top competitor of Fuji Xerox. In the office equipment industry, where the extent and quality of sales/service networks are key factors of success, the strength of Ricoh cannot be ignored in the long run.

pect's view of it. From the very moment the salesman makes his first call till the last moment when the prospect puts his signature on the contract, the salesman's activities are matched step by step by the prospect's corresponding activities. Graphically the relationship may be shown as follows:

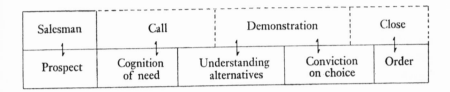

Salesman	Call	Demonstration	Close
Prospect	Cognition of need	Understanding alternatives	Conviction on choice	Order

In other words, the sales cycle is the prospect's response cycle and the salesman's effort should concentrate upon shortening the span between the stage of cognition and the stage of conviction.

At this juncture it may be valuable to consider who it is within the prospect's organization that makes key decisions at different stages of the process. This knowledge is important not only in making sales activities more effective but also in helping other marketing activities set their aims upon the bull's eye.

Recent research sponsored by *Nihon Keizai Shimbun* on office equipment bought by Japanese firms indicates that top management of as many as 33% of respondents makes the buying decisions.[3] Combined with the 30% made by General Affairs departments, it is quite clear that the process is highly centralized and involves a formalized *ringi* system cutting across several levels of management between the point of need and the point of final decision. No wonder most office-equipment salesmen regard these two groups as crucial in landing orders and try in every way possible to gain access to and acceptance by them. (Exhibit 1.)

[3] *Jigyōsha Kōbai Kōdō Chōsa, Jimuki-hen* ('Business Purchasing Pattern Survey, Office Equipment'), Tokyo: Nihon Keizai Shimbun, November 1969, p. 9.

EXHIBIT 1

DECISION PROCESS FOR THE PURCHASING OF OFFICE EQUIPMENT
(1971)

Brand decision	Top management	Special committee	Control	Purchasing	General administration	Planning	Accounting	Marketing	Manufacturing	Others (1)
First decision	4.0	0.8	4.6	4.5	26.6	8.3	19.5	25.5	6.9	21.5
Review	12.9	2.0	2.9	7.5	41.5	2.8	9.2	3.6	1.1	20.3
Detailed vendor analysis	6.5	1.6	2.1	13.9	42.4	2.8	7.3	4.9	1.2	21.1
Decision	33.3	1.5	2.4	6.0	30.0	1.3	6.0	1.9	0.5	19.2

Source: *Nihon Keizai Shimbun*, "Business Purchasing Pattern Survey, Office Equipment," Tokyo: December 1971, p. 8.

Note: (1) "Others" includes three categories: proprietors of small businesses, their employees, and no return.

Chapter Eight. Institutional Promotion

This centralized pattern of business purchasing is nothing new, for it has been confirmed in other studies by *Nihon Keizai Shimbun*: e.g., "Industrial Goods Brand Research" and "Survey on Industrial Goods Purchasing Process," both conducted in 1965.[4] The latter survey, which contains the results of 50 case studies, shows in a diagram of purchasing flow that from at least 10 steps—and therefore 10 different levels of paperwork and as many or more persons—to as many as 30 steps are involved in the typical Japanese purchasing process, depending on the type of products to be purchased or on the type of industry doing the purchasing. The study also indicates that in most cases the final decision is made at the top management level while the General Affairs department acts as the clearing house of requisitions, offering consultancy in brand selection and issuing the actual order to the supplier. (Exhibit 2.)

The former survey, while confirming the same centralized pattern, contains interesting additional information. It reveals that the most influential group in the selection of any brand is not the same at all stages of the purchasing process. At the very outset, for example, most influential over brand selection are the ultimate users, closely followed by the General Affairs department and the immediate supervisors of the users. In the second stage, where the first selection is reviewed and systematically analyzed, the opinion of the General Affairs department carries the heaviest weight, followed closely by that of the ultimate users and their immediate superiors. In the final decision-making process, we know who the right men are.

---

[4] *Seisanzai Meigara Chōsa, Jimuki* ('Industrial Goods Brand Research, Office Equipment'), Tokyo: Nihon Keizai Shimbun, 1965; *Seisanzai Kōbai Purosesu Chōsa* ('Survey on Industrial Goods Purchasing Process'), Tokyo: Nihon Keizai Shimbun, 1965.

EXHIBIT 2

DECISION PROCESS FOR THE PURCHASING OF OFFICE COPIERS
(1965)

	Top management	Special committee	Control	Purchasing	General administration	Planning	Ultimate users	Managers users department	Others
First selection	10.9	0.8	3.0	3.0	31.1	1.7	32.2	14.5	2.9
Review	11.5	1.9	4.3	5.2	33.0	1.0	12.9	26.9	4.0
Decision	45.6	1.1	4.9	3.4	30.3	0.5	1.4	8.8	4.0

Source: *Nihon Keizai Shimbun*, Industrial Goods Brand Research, 1965.

Chapter Eight. Institutional Promotion

Marketing plans

BEFORE the question of product promotion by advertising is discussed in detail, it is probably proper to talk a little about how Fuji Xerox plans its marketing activities, for the nature and direction of promotional activities are fundamentally predetermined by what a company plans for overall marketing.

The marketing planning at Fuji Xerox starts with an assessment of the overall size of the market—number of machines, copies, and establishments graded by number of employees—all this assessed in terms of characteristics by processes of industries, in terms of competitive features available, and in terms of market requirements in different segments of the market. For this purpose the company makes full use of published statistical reports, like the annual spring market survey on the industry. Such reports provide not only up-to-date segmented information on most questions but also extensive and thorough general information.

Given a certain set of products, the next logical step in initiating an effective product development is determining the target market. What is needed is a translation of market requirements into quantitative measurements and a determination of the segments with greatest growth and profit potentials. It is at this stage that the need for creating new markets should become manifest.

Again, target markets can be recognized in terms of industry, applications, or size of establishment. Because the main product of Fuji Xerox is rented rather than sold, the size of establishment, classification by industry, type of operation (head office, plant, or branch, for example), and geography are primary considerations. Very broadly speaking, those establishments, whether private or governmental, with more than 10 employees are regarded as the target market for the main product of Fuji Xerox. Why 10 instead of, say, 50 employees? Because as a result of step one, assessment of the market, the company management is assured that, where there

[175]

are at least 10 employees, there will be a sufficient volume of paper-work to justify the use of the copiers/duplicators which Fuji Xerox markets or plans to market and with a reasonable expectation that Fuji Xerox will command a good 80% coverage of the total poten-tiality of the market.

The next step in marketing planning is the establishment of both long-range and short-range objectives. Such objectives should include the relating of marketing objectives to separately decided corporate objectives both quantitative and qualitative and the establishment of profitability objectives, or fixing the rate of market penetration in those areas heretofore recognized as the target market. Fuji Xerox has carried this step out most assiduously in a joint effort with Rank Xerox and Xerox Corporation, with the result that a mutually compatible set of objectives has been achieved. Included in this area of consideration are a minimum annual growth rate of 20%, a profit rate of not less than 10%, or a rate of penetration of not less than 50% in prime target markets.

With the market assessed, the target market defined, and a set of marketing objectives established, management must now address itself to the achievement of its objectives. Here final choices must be made on product, pricing, field manpower and organization, sales compensation, and promotional activities.

It goes without saying that though the main product line is not likely to change too easily or too often, emphasis on a certain product within it may from time to time change, however slightly, depending on current competition. A final plan must accordingly allow for such changes by reflecting the choice of other marketing tools like pricing, advertising or sales incentives, and the tone of communication with the market. The plan should include a set of strategies and tactics by which pre-set marketing objectives may be reached. The role and timing of promotional activities should also be specified. Schematically the process may be illustrated as in Exhibit 3.

EXHIBIT 3
MARKETING PLAN

MAJOR DECISIONS

MARKET ASSESSMENT

DEFINING TARGET MARKET

ESTABLISHING MARKETING GOALS

FORMULATING MARKETING PLANS

ACTION

SUB-DECISIONS

Evaluation of markets by:
—industry
—geography
—competitors'size of establishment

Segmenting and evaluating on:
market opportunities in terms
of revenue and profit best suited
for company's capabilities

Establishing objectives re:
—revenue and profit
—market penetration
—qualitative objectives

Choices of marketing tools:
—product mix
—pricing
—manpower and organization
—promotional mix
—sales compensation

Promoting "Xerox"

FUJI XEROX is carrying out a variety of promotional activities, all of which are designed to initiate the movement of the goods and services the company provides in the market place. In the office-equipment industry—or the industrial-goods industry in general, for that matter—it is widely accepted that, whether the products are rented or purchased outright, personal selling plays the single most important role in the sales process and the significance of what is usually called house sales is extremely small. If personal selling is set aside for the moment, non-human promotional activities may be discussed more objectively.

The role of product promotion in industrial-goods marketing is different from product promotion in the pharmaceutical, cosmetic, and electric-appliance industries, where the points of sale are usually centered in thousands of retail outlets scattered all over the country and where non-human promotional activities—advertising or P.O.P. promotion, for instance—play a highly aggressive role. The fundamental objective of non-human promotional activities in industrial-goods marketing is to make each step in the personal selling process more effective—hopefully, in the short run, resulting in a shortened sales cycle per salesman, and, in the long run, establishing the company's image in the prospect/customer's minds most favorably, thus making the long-term marketing effort most productive regardless of the products or services it may wish to provide in the future. The non-human promotional activities in the office-equipment industry have a relatively passive role to play as compared with those in the industries cited earlier, at least with respect to the immediate movement of goods or services.

SETTING OBJECTIVES

ALL marketing activities have to be supported by the logical setting of objectives, and promotional activities are no exception to this rule.

In earlier years setting promotional objectives at Fuji Xerox was neither logical nor systematic. Without really knowing the full implications of the capabilities and destination of the company, management was not at all clear about what it should promote. Most people outside the company did not know how to pronounce "Xerox"; many people wrote the name "Zerox"; and many people thought the product was some sort of cough tablet. Nobody had even heard of renting an office copier, to say nothing of a copier that produces copies on ordinary paper.

Today, however, pronounced and spelled correctly, Xerox means a number of things to the public: copies, copiers, a rental system, quality service, information systems, the information explosion, and so on and on. Fuji Xerox has grown into a billion dollar corporation commanding a leading position in the Japanese office copying/duplicating industry. It has diversified in such areas as computers, education, publishing, and even medical diagnostics, as often reported in various publications. Not only does Xerox more or less epitomize the office equipment of today and tomorrow, but also, as the business has grown, the amount of information about it available to the public and therefore the versatility of its corporate image have also grown.

Earlier objectives

Thus, based on the initial market reception its marketing effort met in the very early days, the promotional objectives of Fuji Xerox were set as follows:

—To promulgate the name of Xerox
—To educate the market about the rental system
—To establish the Xerox image as that of the best copier.

These were all short-term objectives, because it was felt rather ridiculous to discuss longer-term objectives without having dealt with more immediate market obstacles. In time, as the company's short-term objectives were met, other short-term objectives were added, such as promoting a wider range of products, faster machines, new pricing schemes, and the like.

Not until about 1965 were long-term objectives defined. By then it was fairly well understood where the Xerox group was headed. It was aiming for growth into a first-rate information processing business with great emphasis on graphic communications and on quality of service. Accordingly, the objective of establishing the corporate image as

—progressive,
—excellent in services,
—innovative, and
—reliable

was added. Institutional advertising was started only in 1966/1967. About this time also advertisements showing that Fuji Xerox, though a joint venture, was a Japanese, not a foreign, company began to appear. In addition to establishing the corporate image as international, and therefore progressive, it had become increasingly apparent that the company's recruitment effort required some modification, for the kind of people the company wanted to hire hesitated more often than not on the false assumption that Fuji Xerox was a foreigner-riddled company.

Objectives confirmed

Today Fuji Xerox operates according to three main sets of promotional objectives, classified by time spans, in the belief that they are necessary prerequisites for meeting today's marketing requirements and for creating an atmosphere favorable to fully effective operations. The objectives are classified as follows:

i) Short range: for the current year's operations
—promoting current range of products
—stress on product features superior to those of the competition, such as speed, cost, versatility, and automaticity

ii) Medium range: for the next year or two
—promoting newer products
—promoting benefits of the marketing system, such as rentals, avoidance of obsolescence risk, flexibility in product mix, etc.
—promoting immediate customer services

iii) Long range: five years or more ahead
—promoting research and development
—promoting new, as yet unrevealed processes or products
—promoting possibilities of a wider range of corporate participation in the information industry

Chapter Eight. Institutional Promotion

—promoting the corporate image of progressiveness, innovation, and quality service

PROMOTIONAL MIX

THE cited objectives, if they are to be met, have to be matched by appropriate and effective means of promotion. In allocating roles to different promotional media such as advertising, direct sales promotion, publicity, or even the personal selling by the sales representatives themselves, Fuji Xerox uses the allocation table given as Exhibit 4.

With some interest, this table can be compared with Exhibit 5 indicating the relative weight of effectiveness different promotional means play in each step of the sales process. The chart derives from a survey carried out by IBM in the United States with respect to marketing its character-sensing equipment. This chart correlates quite closely with both the sales process pattern and the respective roles different promotional means play in Fuji Xerox. Moreover, it correlates regardless of the point of view—whether from that of a short-term sales process of some single product, in which case the applicability is obvious, or from that of the longer-term marketing activities of the company as a whole. If one looks at this process from the latter point of view it is possible to regard the first one and one-half steps as long/medium range and the next two and one-half as short range. It seems clear also that the Fuji Xerox table parallels the relative effectiveness of objectives as indicated in the IBM chart.

Based on the type of recognition involved, the following promotional activities are carried out at Fuji Xerox today:

a) Personal selling
   i) Sales by geographical territory
   ii) Sales by size (and importance) of customers
   iii) Sales by type of industries (finance, industry, government, etc.)
   iv) Promotional activities by Customer Service Officers

EXHIBIT 4
EFFECTIVENESS OF PROMOTIONAL MEDIA
AT FUJI-XEROX

Media \ Objectives	Short range	Medium range	Long range
Personal selling	◎		
Sales promotion	◎	○	
Institutional Ad / Product Ad	○ / ◎	◎ / ○	◎ / △
Publicity	△	○	◎

Notes: ◎ Most effective
○ Effective
△ Sometimes effective

EXHIBIT 5
EFFECTIVENESS OF PROMOTIONAL MEDIA
(character-sensing equipment)

	Cognition	Understanding	Conviction	Action
Personal selling				
Advertising				
Sales promotion				
Publicity				

Source: Tasaburō Kobayashi, *Gendai Kōkoku Nyūmon* ('Introduction to Contemporary Advertising'), Tokyo: Diamond, 1969, p. 63.

[182]

b) Advertising (see Exhibit 6)

c) Sales promotion

   i) National trade shows
      Tokyo Business Show, Osaka Business Show,
      National Microfilm Association Show, etc.

   ii) Local trade shows

   iii) Private shows

   iv) Xerox Lecture/Seminar Services
      Xerox Management Seminar,
      Major Account Information Seminar,
      Engineering Systems Seminar,
      Duplicating Systems Seminar, etc.

d) Publicity

   i) "Xerox Knowledge-In" at the Sony Building

   ii) Graphics Magazine

The total cost of these promotional expenses (excluding personal selling) and the percentage of the company's total revenue they represent are shown in Exhibit 6.

EXHIBIT 6
PROMOTIONAL EXPENSES
(1965–1971)

	1965	1966	1967	1968	1969	1970	1971
Sales promotion	31%	20%	22%	26%	16%	11%	13%
Product ad	42	35	37	33	32	23	31
Institutional ad	27	35	39	39	48	60	47
Publicity	—	10	2	2	4	6	9
Total	100%	100%	100%	100%	100%	100%	100%
Against revenue	4.4	3.3	3.1	2.9	2.4	1.9	2.1
Amount	100	126	176	232	317	286*	416

* For seven months only because of a change in the term of the fiscal year.

Advertising

OF all promotional mixes, advertising has played the most important role, except for personal selling, at Fuji Xerox.

As already indicated, the function of non-human promotional activities including advertising at Fuji Xerox is, in the short run, to make personal selling more effective and shorter in cycle and, in the long run, to create an atmosphere which will help make future marketing activities more effective—in brief, image-building.

Another reason for the importance advertising plays at Fuji Xerox is that the company operates through direct sales only. Because its marketing organization is built on this direct sales system and because such a system makes it harder to recruit and employ *en masse* competent professional sales skills, the company's sales coverage on the horizontal level is limited as compared with the sales coverage of other companies that depend mostly on route-selling and employ deep strata of distributors and retailers. Fuji Xerox needs something to fill this competitive sales gap, at least for the time being, for at present it is not filled by either personal selling or any other short-term promotional measure.

In addition to facilitating the marketing process of the company, advertising activities play another major role, that of attracting workforce. In an age of increasing labor shortage this role is rapidly growing in importance. Apparently because its promotional campaigns appeal to a wide spectrum of people, Fuji Xerox has attracted a number of potential employees through such means, most markedly through mass advertisements and such programs as the "Knowledge-In" held at the Sony Building in Tokyo. Both new graduates of universities and those employees coming to Fuji Xerox from other firms have cited the company's promotional activities as key inducements that have brought them to its door. Although they cite a number of reactions, the most positive has been their sense of innovative and refreshing management postures in the company as inferred from innovative and refreshing techniques of promotion. Concretely, they have mentioned internationalism, progressiveness, freedom of work, flexible organization, youth, and the like as factors they have learned to associate with the company through its promotional activities. Given the fact that these people have not come to the company to seek jobs in advertising, this experience casts a clear light upon the value of promotional programs in building workforce and overall organization. Indeed, where recruitment of employees is concerned, Fuji Xerox has had a more remarkable response from the advertisement of its regular product and the promotion of the company itself than from its straightforward advertisements soliciting recruits.

CHOICE AMONG ADVERTISING MEDIA

As Xerox products are many and have definite market segments to aim at, the choice among the advertising media that Xerox uses inclines heavily toward mass media in general. The selling of industrial goods requires more persuasion and understanding than a mere "buying urge", and therefore Fuji Xerox tends to put greater emphasis on print than on other media. In general, the print media are considered most effective in directing persuasive information to those segments of the market the company wants to reach.

Print media are divided between newspapers and magazines, but the former far outvalue the latter. The relative weight among different advertising media is given in Exhibit 7. The flexibility of mixes (national vs. local) and the high acceptability by the public of newspapers as dependable channels of information make this still today the most relatively economical means of advertising.

The choice among advertising media is greatly influenced by the company's target audience, which is very carefully selected, especially with respect to the people who exert influence over buying processes. As long as the fundamental role of advertising is to assist salesmen in successfully conducting their sales effort,

EXHIBIT 7
RELATIVE WEIGHT AMONG ADVERTISING MEDIA
(1965-1971)

	1965	1966	1967	1968	1969	1970	1971
National papers	34%	35%	36%	36%	33%	43%	32%
Local papers	11	17	19	21	19	15	15
General magazines	7	8	10	14	10	9	10
Trade journals	2	2	2	4	1	1	2
Direct mail	4	3	3	4	4	2	1
TV	42	35	30	21	33	30	40
Radio	—	—	—	—	—	—	—
Total	100%	100%	100%	100%	100%	100%	100%

the selection is paramount from the point of view of marshalling all promotional activities for a maximum degree of effectiveness.

At Fuji Xerox the target audience has long been the so-called decision-makers in businesses, and the choice of media has long been based on this fact. Heavy usage of such print media as *Nihon Keizai Shimbun* or *Asahi* in newspapers and *President* or *Nikkei Business* in magazines is an evident testimonial to this fact. Decision-makers concerned with the purchase of office equipment are known to be prime subscribers to these publications.

Recently, however, a fresh probe into this well-established policy is being attempted at Fuji Xerox, prompted specifically by the realization of one recent phenomenon, the increasing shortage of office manpower and its concomitant implications for the purchasing of industrial goods. The probe centers around the hypothesis that the increasing scarcity of office manpower will eventually make acceptance by office workers the single most important factor influencing management's decision to purchase some types of industrial goods. Fuji Xerox management believes that the copiers and duplicators that it markets fall into such a category because of simple human involvement. If this is so, the hypothesis continues, promotional activities will have to be redirected at the decision-makers of tomorrow who, in Fuji Xerox's view, are modern youth. Depending on the outcome of this probe, it will not be necessary to add, the choice of advertising media in the future may have to undergo a rather thorough re-examination.

PROCESS OF ADVERTISING ACTIVITIES

THE process of advertising activities at Fuji Xerox, as elsewhere, begins with a definition of goals. Naturally, corporate objectives and, therefore, marketing objectives, both short-term and long-term, must be defined beforehand. Although easily verbalized, the task is not very easy, for the validity and clarity of defined advertising objectives largely determine the measurement of effectiveness. As stated before, the advertising objectives of Fuji Xerox in its earlier days were to improve the corporate image, to establish public awareness of the product, and to impress the market with the view that the Xerox 914 was the best copier available anywhere. All the company's advertising activities were then designed to meet these objectives. Today in areas like Kyushu, Shikoku, Chugoku, or Hokkaido/Tohoku the company's advertising has retained some of these original objectives as the advertisements in local newspapers in these areas clearly reflect. In short, the corporate image and public awareness of the product still leave much room for improvement in these areas.

On the other hand, the company's cosmopolitan markets spearheaded by Tokyo have acquired a very high percentage of awareness both of the corporate image and the product, and further stress on basic objectives is a highly expensive marginal exercise. Based on the belief that the public in these areas are more interested in what will come next and what Xerox's rental system will provide them with in a few years' time, a greater emphasis is laid on institutional and conceptual advertising.

Once advertising objectives are set, creative goals must be established and that set of media must be chosen which promises the greatest degree of penetration and effectiveness. Here the role of advertising agencies deserves serious attention. At Fuji Xerox once advertising objectives are clear (and usually they are jointly decided by Fuji Xerox and its advertising agency) the rest of the process—namely, the creative operations, selection of and dealings with a particular media, and the designing of an effectiveness-measuring system—is all done by the agency.

THE ROLE OF THE ADVERTISING AGENCY

AT Fuji Xerox two advertising agencies are used. One, very large and resourceful, looks after newspaper and television media, and the other, relatively small but very creative, looks after magazine advertising. At one time Fuji Xerox employed about five agencies for one purpose or the other, all either small or medium in size; but in 1966 the number was reduced to three (one of which then looked after television only), and finally, in 1967, to two.

The essential roles which Fuji Xerox expects of its agencies are creative resourcefulness and the effective purchase of space. Unlike some other modern corporations, Fuji Xerox does not believe in using the agencies to help the company in establishing broader marketing strategies or objectives. The company strongly believes that setting its own corporate objectives and choosing the most effective marketing strategies for achieving them are the job of company management alone. By contrast, creative work is definitely the forte of trained advertising staffs. Company executives cannot become creative experts in art and psychology. (Exhibit 8.)

At Fuji Xerox each year, about a couple of months before the start of the new fiscal year, a joint advertising-strategy meeting is held by the company's advertising department and the key executives of the advertising agencies the company uses. Here the new year's marketing strategies and objectives are clearly spelled out, and any question about them is answered. The advertising budget containing allotments to different media is also made known at this meeting, and the agencies are asked to make plans of action in accord with the budget.

EXHIBIT 8
COOPERATION BETWEEN THE COMPANY
AND THE ADVERTISING AGENCY

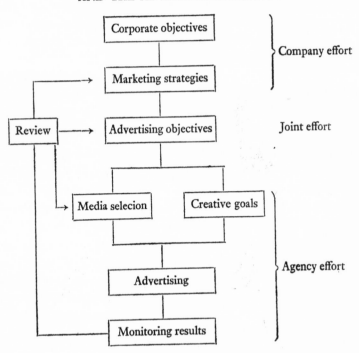

Several weeks later the company's advertising department holds further advertising-planning meetings with the two agencies retained, in order to decide on the presentation the agencies propose for year-long newspaper/magazine advertising programmes.

A joint meeting is also held in the middle of the year in order to review what has been done and to discuss and confirm the plans for the rest of the year. From time to time meetings are held in which advertising is planned or reviewed on the basis of media. Very often the product planning and promotion executives attend these meetings in order to contribute their views of advertising effectiveness that they have observed through experience closer to the scene. The advertising company executives, together with members of their creative staffs, are free to attend most of Fuji Xerox's marketing meetings.

ORGANIZATION

WITHIN Fuji Xerox, advertising and publicity activities are carried out by the Marketing Operations Division and the Corporate Planning Department, and short-term sales promotion activities by the Sales Promotion Department. The organizational set-up is shown in Exhibit 9.

EXHIBIT 9
ORGANIZATIONAL SET-UP

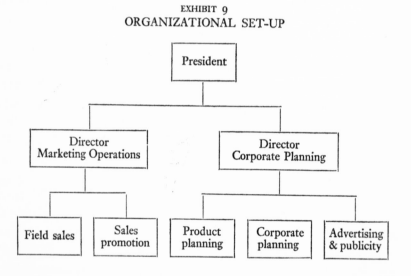

Broadly speaking, the main responsibility of the director of Marketing Operations is to meet the current year's marketing objectives, whereas that of the director of Corporate Planning is to plan and to control corporate activities both short-term and long-term, but with a greater emphasis on the latter. The company's advertising fulfills both short-term and long-term objectives but a greater emphasis has been placed in recent years on medium-long-term objectives. Because of the close relationship that exists between marketing operations and advertising, this department is placed in the Marketing Operations Division.

The Advertising Department is further divided by media as in Exhibit 10.

EXHIBIT 10
THE ADVERTISING DEPARTMENT

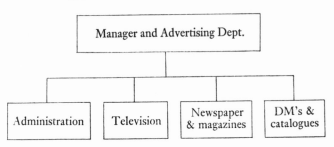

As was said earlier, in the overall advertising process the role the company's advertising department plays is that of planning advertising objectives and budget by media and of controlling and measuring their effectiveness. Members of the advertising staff are therefore all planners and not doers.

MEASURING EFFECTIVENESS

As with most advertisers, Fuji Xerox finds the measuring of effectiveness in the advertising process most difficult and yet most urgently needed. Though in principle effectiveness is measured against pre-set objectives and goals rather than against sales results (machine installation, copy volume, or the revenue), the company urgently needs a consistent system of objective measurement of effectiveness on a continuing basis. At the moment the company employs a monitoring system that sounds out the effectiveness of film commercials on television, and one of its agencies makes an annual survey of the effectiveness of the company's advertising and of the quality and penetration of its corporate image. A test is now being conducted in Kyushu and Chugoku to measure the effectiveness of vastly increased newspaper advertising on direct sales in these areas as against the previous level and against that of other local areas with similar economic indicators.

For reference, the trend of public awareness of the company's product revealed in annual research projects is shown in Exhibit 11.

EXHIBIT 11

BRAND AWARENESS AND CORPORATE IMAGE
OF FUJI XEROX
(1965–1971)

	1965	1966	1967	1968	1969	1970	(%) 1971
As a company							
	—	—	81 (91)	98 (98)	93 (98)	93 (98)	97 (98)
As a copier manufacturer							
A	4 (75)	18 (60)	17 (71)	23 (43)	44 (37)	38 (40)	45 (39)
B	33 (93)	45 (80)	45 (78)	53 (65)	68 (68)	67 (74)	76 (81)
C	50 (98)	70 (95)	81 (95)	80 (86)	88 (84)	95 (94)	98 (97)
As the best copier							
	25 (24)	35 (33)	43 (25)	52 (17)	42 (18)	53 (15)	58 (11)
Strong points in corporate image							
Good products	—	o	o	o	o	o	o
Growth stock	—	o	o	o	o	o	o
Good R & D	—	—	—	—	o	o	o
Reliability	—	—	—	o	o	o	o
Progressiveness	—	o	o	o	o	o	o
Internationality	—	—	o	o	o	o	o
Effective advertising	—	—	o	o	o	o	o

Note: (1) Figures in (   ) are for Fuji Xerox's largest competitor.

(2) A=Percentage of people who quoted Fuji Xerox *first* when asked about the copier manufacturers they knew.

B=Percentage of people who quoted Fuji Xerox among the copier manufacturers they knew.

C=Percentage of people who recognized Fuji Xerox as a copier manufacturer when asked if they knew Fuji Xerox.

Chapter Eight. Institutional Promotion

Though we know the corporate image of Fuji Xerox has both broadened and improved over the years, as research figures testify, it is still uncertain how much promotional activities alone can contribute to making, maintaining, improving, or even damaging the corporate image.

Mr. T. Levitt, for instance, referring to Shoaf's study of emotional factors in industrial purchasing, says as follows:

> "[Hence] the company is assumed to have an image which the salesman merely reflects, but presumably his failure to reflect it properly will cause the image to change. The question of where the image comes from in the first place is for the most part company advertising. But specifically advertising of the company, not primarily advertising of its products. Thus one interpreter of the Shoaf study declares that as time goes on the importance of making the market aware of a company's reliability or capabilities of enterprise transcends that of promoting the product's characteristics."[5]

It is strongly believed at Fuji Xerox that the corporate image is the result of an accumulated corporate behavior and effort most clearly epitomized in the quality of product, services, and human representations and that promotional activities exist only to facilitate these components of corporate performance.

Should a company marketing a foreign made or designed product (or services) be doing something very different about creating a favorable corporate image? It is not likely. Too often the dominant Japanese attitude that singularly favors *Japanese* products is blamed by foreign firms or firms marketing foreign products for a bad image. It is sometimes claimed that such an image is created in the Japanese market merely *because* the corporation and its product are foreign.

[5] T. Levitt, *Industrial Purchasing Behavior*, Boston, Mass.: Harvard Business School, Division of Research, p. 25.

Objectively considered, however, if there is any Japanese hesitancy about buying foreign products it may very well be due to inconveniences in servicing, the difficulty of getting spare parts, some deficiency in product configuration, and probably the expense of performance. If a corporate image built up in Japan is very different from that in the home country, the fact calls for some re-examination of corporate behavior, management, products, services, or employees, in the light of Japanese assessment.

Although various promotional activities and advertising agencies exist primarily to help make the awareness of overall corporate behavior clearer and fuller, they cannot change the corporate behavior itself, which in actuality creates the ultimate corporate image.

Index

Index

Index